THINKING
ABOUT RELIGION

Thinking
About Religion

A Philosophical Introduction to Religion

RICHARD L. PURTILL
Western Washington State College
Bellingham, Washington

PRENTICE-HALL, INC., Englewood Cliffs, New Jersey 07632

Library of Congress Cataloging in Publication Data

PURTILL, RICHARD L. (date).
   Thinking about religion.

   Bibliography: p. 153
   Includes indexes.
   1. Religion—Philosophy.   I. Title.
BL51.P88   200'.1   77-13616
ISBN   0-13-917724-8

Printed in the United States of America

10   9   8   7   6   5   4   3   2   1

PRENTICE-HALL INTERNATIONAL, INC., *London*
PRENTICE-HALL OF AUSTRALIA PTY. LIMITED, *Sydney*
PRENTICE-HALL OF CANADA, LTD., *Toronto*
PRENTICE-HALL OF INDIA PRIVATE LIMITED, *New Delhi*
PRENTICE-HALL OF JAPAN, INC., *Tokyo*
PRENTICE-HALL OF SOUTHEAST ASIA PTE. LTD., *Singapore*
WHITEHALL BOOKS LIMITED, *Wellington, New Zealand*

This book is dedicated to
G. K. Chesterton
and
C. S. Lewis
whose writings began my own
thinking about religion.

Contents

10

LIFE AFTER DEATH:

What Would It Be Like?

Preface

This book is intended for introductory classes in philosophy of religion, and also for introductory classes with such titles as "Introduction to Religion" or "Religious Thought." It covers, however, a somewhat different range of material than the usual introductory book in either of these areas. The usual philosophy of religion book covers a fairly narrow range of topics—arguments for and against the existence of God, the relationship between faith and reason, the nature of religious language, perhaps something about problems connected with life after death. I have found—and other teachers have told me that their experience has been similar—that present-day students have certain difficulties with this range of topics.

The difficulties arise from the fact that many students no longer come to a class in philosophy of religion with any real background in religion or experience of religious belief. Even those who claim to be adherents of one of the major Western religious groups—Catholicism, Protestantism, Judaism—cannot be counted on to have much knowledge of the beliefs or practices of their religion. There are no doubt many reasons for this—changes in family life, different approaches to religious instruction, a generally more emotional and less intellectual approach to religion in recent generations. But the practical result of this lack of knowledge is that the background which is presupposed in many discussions of philosophy of religion is lacking in many students.

Students today have a wide range of perplexities about religion, many of them theological or historical rather than philosophical. It would seem, then, that the historical or comparative approach taken by many "Introduction to Religion" textbooks would be what they need. But this approach, too, has its difficulties. Students want and need more than a merely factual presentation of what religious beliefs have been held at various times and places. They need to understand why anyone holds any religious belief and to consider whether there are grounds for holding one set of religious beliefs rather than another.

The topics I have covered in this book are those which I have found to create the most interest and cause the most discussion when they have come up in class. Many of them are topics which have been suggested by students themselves when given the opportunity. But the philosopher of religion will find most of his standard themes discussed, although perhaps in a new way. The teacher of introductory surveys in religion will also find many of the themes he has been treating in historical or comparative surveys discussed in a somewhat different way. This book could, and ideally should, be supplemented by a good book of readings in original sources.

There is, unfortunately, no single book of readings which adequately covers all of the topics discussed in this book. At the end of each chapter I have given references to selections from two of the best books of readings now available, and also to another introductory book which covers many of the same topics as this one, but in a somewhat more technical fashion. I have tried to treat the topics considered here as nontechnically as possible without sacrificing accuracy and depth. I have used the same technique I used in an earlier book: introducing each chapter with a story or parable designed to arouse student interest and to raise questions which lead into the discussion of the topic of the chapter.

Several matters of style need brief comments. In many contexts I have used the rather vague and general term "religious believer" rather than precise terms such as "theist," for a variety of reasons. Often it was because I wanted to refer not just to those who believe in God, but to those who accept some definite set of religious beliefs, for example, some form of Christianity or Judaism. Sometimes I wanted to mark the contrast between mere intellectual agreement that God exists, and a commitment to God. In most cases the context makes it clear what I have in mind, and where necessary I have added qualifications, e.g., Western or Eastern, Christian or Jewish religious believer.

In references to the God of Judeo-Christian religious belief I have kept to the traditional masculine pronouns and I have capitalized pronouns referring to God, not because I think either convention of great religious importance, but simply for the sake of clarity.

In matters of substance as well as in matters of style I have tried not to offend the sensibilities of any of my readers; no doubt I have sometimes failed and for this I apologize in advance. The old saying that "theological hatreds are the worst kind" (*odium theologicum est odium pessimum*) is too often true, but I have tired to discuss views with which I disagree with charity as well as clarity. I have tried to be as even-handed as possible, but no doubt on many points my own views will be obvious enough.

If any set of religious beliefs is justified, the importance of knowing that it is can hardly be exaggerated. If no set of religious beliefs is justified, that in itself would be a vitally important fact. Such questions deserve the most serious and careful thinking. This book is intended as an aid to such thinking.

My thanks to the Bureau for Faculty Research at Western Washington University for assistance in the preparation of the book and to Mrs. Ann Drake and Mrs. Mary Sutterman who did the typing. Thanks also to Norwell F. Therien, Jr. and Jean Behr of Prentice-Hall. Special thanks to all the friends and colleagues with whom I have argued and discussed philosophy of religion, especially Charles Hartshorne, Alvin Plantinga, Robert Richman, Albert Wald, David Freeman, Donald Zeyl, Stephen Schwarz, Stanley Kane, Grace Dyck, Milton Hunnex, Tom Talbott and Del Ratzsch.

Religion Today:

"Why Don't We Believe Anymore . . . ?"

1

The steady rattle of Joanna's typewriter slowed and then stopped. She reached for a packet of cigarettes on the desk and as she did so heard a rustle of movement near the door. Peering out into the dark room beyond the bright circle made by her desk lamp, she saw her daughter curled in a chair across the room, her shoes on the floor and her feet folded under her now crumpled skirt. "Why Phil," said Joanna, "how long have you been there? I didn't hear you come in."

Philomena smiled as she said, "You were typing so hard you didn't hear me," but something in her voice and a sort of tension in her seemingly relaxed posture told Joanna that there were problems. Only to be expected perhaps. This was Philomena's first visit with her father since Robert had remarried.

"How was Daddy?" Joanna asked. "Was Sharon nice?" Nice. Nice to Philomena. Nice to Robert. Joanna wasn't quite sure herself what she meant or what she felt.

"She was fine," said Philomena. "Don't worry, Mother, lots of my friends have parents who are divorced and remarried. It isn't that that's bothering me."

Joanna waited to hear what had been more upsetting for Phil than seeing her father with his new wife. When Philomena said, "We went to church this morning," and stopped, Joanna didn't at first understand. "But dear," she said, "they didn't . . ."

Philomena shook her head, "Make me go? Preach at me? No, Mother, it was just a thing they do, a family thing. I went along just to see. . . ." Her voice became a little shriller and Joanna thought, "Here it comes. But what did come was unexpected. "Mother, when I was little you and I and Daddy went to church. Why don't we go anymore? And it's not just going to church—why don't we believe in God anymore?"

"Well, it had to come sometime," thought Joanna, casting a half-regretful glance at the unfinished page in her typewriter and tilting the desk lampshade a little to give more light to the rest of the room. "I haven't talked much about this to you, Phil, because I knew that Robert had started going to church again when he met Sharon and I didn't want to . . ."

Philomena interrupted her. "Influence me? You've done that already, Mother. I don't believe any more than you do. I didn't feel anything in church. But there were people there, people from the university and just ordinary people, like the man from our gas station. They must believe in it. Lots of people seem to, but lots of people, like us, seem not to. What's the difference? Why did you stop believing in God?"

Joanna tried to be honest. "Maybe I just drifted away, kitten," she said, unconsciously calling Philomena by an old pet name. "But when I look back I think there were several things that made me stop believing. When I was at the university I had a philosophy class where we talked about arguments for God and some of them sounded fairly convincing. But they never seemed to convince anyone who didn't believe in God already. Then there was the war, right after your Daddy and I got married—so many people killed, so many horrible things happening. It just didn't seem to be the kind of thing a good God would allow. Then I suppose the kind of work I do, the technical writing, has had an effect too. The scientist's world, the technician's world, doesn't seem to have much room for God."

Philomena looked thoughtful but Joanna was glad to see that she was more relaxed now. "Those aren't reasons for me, I guess," Philomena said. "I never thought about arguing over God's existence. I always thought of belief as a sort of personal decision. Your war, the one Daddy was in, was over before I was born, and I was still in high school when the Vietnam one ended. And I'm not a scientific kind of person. To me it seems like losing my belief in God was part of . . . was part of our family breaking up. And choosing to stay with you, and knowing you didn't believe . . ." She looked at her mother as if asking for something, perhaps approval or reassurance.

But Joanna felt, unexpectedly, a little frightened and almost annoyed with Philomena. "Darling," she said, "one thing I am sure about is that you can't let another person, no matter how close to you, make up your mind for you on a thing like religion. It's as important and as personal a choice as getting married—or unmarried." Joanna was annoyed to find that her voice hadn't stayed quite steady. She swallowed and went on. "Now that you've started thinking about this you should go on until you're satisfied in your own mind. I'll help you if I can, but please don't try to lean on me *or* on Daddy or make it a matter of loyalty to either one of us. You've grown up enough to make up your own mind on a thing as important as this. If I've brought you up properly you'll be able to make a good decision on your own."

Philomena got up and came over to her mother. She leaned over and kissed her on the check. "I think you've done a pretty good job of bringing me up, Mother. And I will keep thinking about it. But right now I'm off to bed. Good night, dear."

Joanna stared after Philomena as she padded barefoot out of the room, leaving her shoes under the chair. I should make her take those up to her closet, thought Joanna. I wonder if I helped any or if I just evaded the issue. Anyway, the next few years won't be boring, whatever else they are. Joanna sighed, lit a cigarette at last, and turned back to her typewriter.

Many people who have abandoned religious belief "drift away," as Joanna put it, or are influenced by personal factors like those mentioned by Philomena. But many of them would cite reasons like those mentioned by Joanna—the failure of arguments for the existence of God, the apparently pointless suffering in the world, the seeming incompatibility of science and religion. We will be looking at objections of these kinds. But before even beginning this task we must stop and ask ourselves whether thinking is a proper approach to religion. There is a widespread view that religious belief is a matter of "personal decision," as Joanna said, and an equally widespread distrust of thinking or logical argument as an aid to making personal decisions.

The two points can, of course, be separated. How to spend our money or what career to choose are matters of personal decision, but most of us try to think carefully and clearly about such decisions. When we fail to do so we often regret it. But is it even certain that religious belief *is* a matter of personal decision? When something is a matter of personal decision what is right for one person can be wrong for another. Spending money on a new stereo set might be right for you, wrong for me. A career as a college teacher can be right for me, but perhaps wrong for you, and so on. But religion deals with such questions as "Is there a God?" and "Do we continue to exist after death?" And it looks as if the answers to such questions depend on how things are, not on our attitudes or tastes. If we will exist after death, we will exist after death no matter what our present opinions are. If God doesn't exist, then no matter how much we want God to exist, He still doesn't exist.

Most people would admit this, if they thought about it clearly. What people seem to mean when they say that religion is a matter of personal decision is that although the truth or falsity of religious claims depends on the way things are, we cannot know whether religious claims are true or false. Therefore we might as well take whatever point of view appeals to us, and no one can prove that we are wrong.

But when people are asked *why* they are so sure that we cannot know the truth or falsity of religious claims, such as "God exists" or "We will continue to exist after death," they are often unable to give any convincing reasons. Most of them have never given any serious consideration to arguments for and against God's existence or for and against life after death. Why then are they so sure that such questions cannot be settled?

One possible explanation for this common conviction that religious questions cannot be answered is the present-day influence and prestige of science. We tend to take scientific methods of settling questions as a model, or paradigm, for answering questions in other areas. And when we find that questions about the existence of God or about life after death cannot be settled by methods like those of science, we have a tendency to think that they cannot be settled at all.

It is easy enough to point out the weaknesses in this way of thinking. The position that scientific methods are the only methods of settling questions is itself open to dispute, and there does not seem to be any way of proving by the methods of science that only the methods of science can settle disputes. This is not just because of the general difficulty of using any method to support its own adequacy, though this is a part of the difficulty. Imagine someone who claimed that a certain prophet could settle any question, and supported this claim by saying that the prophet had said so, and that settled it! A claim that only scientific methods can settle any question, supported by an appeal to scientific methods, would seem to be equally circular and question-begging.

But it is not clear that there *is* any plausible grounds for saying that scientific methods support the claim that only scientific methods can settle questions. For what are the methods of science? Roughly speaking, the formation of precise hypotheses from which we can deduce consequences which can be checked by experiment or observation. If the consequences deduced from the hypothesis check out experimentally or observationally, the hypothesis is confirmed; if they do not, then the hypothesis is disproved. But there does not seem to be any experiment we can perform or observation we could make which would confirm or disconfirm the hypothesis that only scientific methods can settle questions.

However, though the inability of science to establish its own methods as the only ones for settling questions is an important point, bringing out this point does not entirely do away with the feeling that questions which cannot be settled by science must therefore be only matters of personal choice. Perhaps this is because people do know that the methods of science provide a generally trustworthy method of settling certain questions, but many people do not know of any other method which is similarly trustworthy. If science is the only *known* method of settling questions satisfactorily, then the question as to whether it is the only such method that exists seems merely theoretical. So the question in many people's mind is, "If you cannot settle a question scientifically, how *can* you settle it?"

The broadest and most general answer to this question is, "By considering the evidence on both sides of the question and seeing which side is stronger." When we put it in this way we can see that not all evidence is scientific evidence; there is historical evidence, legal evidence, the evidence of our own experience. Of course, we can interpret "observation and experiment" so widely as to make any kind of weighing of evidence "scientific" in a very extended sense, but if we do this, "scientific method" merely becomes a misleading synonym for "considering evidence."

Someone might grant everything we have said so far but argue in this way: "Whether or not we have other ways of settling questions, science is one way and has settled some questions. And the body of information science has discovered leaves no room for God or life after death. Science is incompatible with religion or at least makes religion unnecessary." Persons who argue in this way may be thinking of apparent incompatibilities between particular religious beliefs and particular scientific discoveries, some of which we will discuss later. But they may be thinking of something more general.

To many people it seems that the progress of science has gradually eliminated what might be called the "personal element" in nature. It seems to them that what has happened historically is something like this: primitive man started out by believing in a multitude of spirits, personal or quasi-personal beings whose actions accounted for natural phenomena such as rain or thunder. As human beings learned more about nature they discovered the mechanisms behind such phenomena and no longer needed to account for them by the action of spirits. A belief in a being or beings who regulated the course of nature in general survived these early successes of science, but it seems to many people nowadays that the continued progress of science has given us a picture of the universe which is self-contained, which needs no explanations in terms of a God or gods. Finally, even the idea of man as spiritual or personal seems to be threatened by modern discourse in physiology and psychology. Human beings are now seen by many as merely highly conditioned animals or as flesh-and-blood computers.

At this point we might ask ourselves if the elimination of the personal element has not progressed to the point of absurdity. It might be true that certain phenomena we thought due to personal agencies are in fact the result of impersonal forces. But could we ever discover that the actions of human beings like you and me are entirely the result of impersonal forces, that, so to speak, persons are not personal? Some people in fact seem to claim that the answer to this question is yes; and that the traditional ideas of human nature must be seriously modified or even eliminated. The pros and cons of this question are rather complex; for the moment let us consider the alleged elimination by science of the idea of a personal God.

Not much weight can be put on the mere "argument from progression" that because we have eliminated a multiplicity of gods we must therefore end up with no God at all. Not all progressions can be reasonably carried to zero. Consider the joke about the miserly farmer who fed his long suffering cow less and less each day; but just when he thought that he had weaned the cow from eating altogether, the unfortunate animal died. Many cows (and people) could get along with less food, but they cannot get along with none. So showing that we do not need as many gods as early man believed does not show that we need no gods at all; that must be argued on its merits.

But the supporter of the view that science has eliminated the need for God can argue as follows: Science explains phenomena in terms of laws or theories and explains those laws and theories in terms of higher level laws and theories. At no stage does science need to bring in God or any other personal agent. Indeed, if anyone did bring in God as an explanation of some phenomenon his explanation would be regarded as unscientific by the very fact of God's being brought in.

However, there is an important ambiguity in this last claim. An explanation may be unscientific because it contradicts or conflicts with scientific knowledge. But an explanation can be unscientific in another sense—by being a different *kind* of explanation, not scientific but, for example, philosophical or theological. Thus to say that an explanation which brings in God is thereby unscientific may merely be to say that it is some other kind of explanation. A court case may be stopped not for any legal reason but because the judge has had a heart attack; the explanation of the stoppage is medical, not legal. But the stoppage is not nonlegal in the sense of being *illegal*. Similarly, a nonscientific explanation is not necessarily antiscientific, but unfortunately we use the word "unscientific" to mean both "antiscientific" and "not scientific but something else."

One might, of course, claim that to give a theological or other nonscientific explanation is always to give an antiscientific explanation. But this sounds suspiciously like the claim, for which we have so far seen no support, that *only* scientific method can settle questions. In some situations a scientific explanation may compete with a nonscientific explanation, but even where this happens we cannot automatically assume that the scientific explanation is to be preferred. Perhaps it sometimes, or always, is to be preferred; but we would need an argument for this contention.

However, there may be cases where the choice is not between a scientific explanation and a nonscientific explanation, but between a nonscientific explanation and no explanation at all. Consider, for example, the apparent order and understandability of the universe. Philosophical and theological explanations have been given for the apparent orderliness of the universe and for our ability to understand the universe. But since science presupposes this order and understandability, it is hard to see how there could be a scientific explanation for it, *or* how there could be a scientific argument for there being no explanation of this apparent order and understandability *or* a scientific argument for or against any nonscientific explanation of it. (Similarly, there can be legal explanations of particular laws and procedures, but not a legal explanation of the existence of laws.)

The existence of science as embodying successful techniques for dealing with the universe and apparently successful techniques for understanding the universe can be taken as a piece of data: a fact which itself needs to be explained. The religious believer has an explanation for the success of science; in his view the universe is orderly and understandable because it has been made by an intelligent Being and made in such a way that we can understand it and learn from it about its Maker. Just as we can reasonably expect a book written by an intelligent author to be understandable to the audience for whom it was written, so it is reasonable to expect that a universe made by God will be understandable to those made in God's "image and likeness." This is precisely the position of many religious believers. They would claim that their world-view can account for the success of science, and in addition many religious believers would claim that nonreligious or purely materialistic theories cannot give a plausible explanation for the success of science, or for the apparent order and understandability of the universe.

Two sorts of reply could be made by the nonbeliever to this claim of the believer. One argument might be that the idea of a God as Maker of the universe does *not* explain the apparent order and understandability of the universe or the success of science. The other possible reply by the nonbeliever would be to grant the believer's claim that he has *an* explanation but to claim that there are other equally plausible or more plausible explanations of our success in understanding and controlling nature.

One argument sometimes given to try to show that the religious believer has not really explained the apparent order and understandability of the universe is that the believer, instead of giving a genuine explanation, has merely pushed the difficulty of explaining back one stage. An intelligent God, it is claimed, is just as puzzling as an intelligible universe. If we ask, "Why is the universe orderly and understandable?" and answer that question by bringing in an intelligent Maker of the universe, why cannot we equally ask "Why is God such that He makes an orderly and understandable universe?"

The religious believer will often reply at this point that on his view God is a Being of a special kind. To be God is to have existed always whether anything else exists or not, and to be without limitations or dependencies of any kind. Thus any question about why God has certain characteristics cannot be the question "How did God *get* those characteristics?" (since God would always have had them), or "On what does God depend for having those characteristics?" (since God would be totally independent of anything else). Thus, the ultimate answer to any question about God's characteristics would be that God has those characteristics "essentially" or "by nature" because He is the kind of Being He is.

At this point the objecting unbeliever must make a crucial choice. He can argue against the idea of explaining the characteristics of something by saying that the thing has a certain nature. But if he does that he cannot consistently explain the apparent order and understandability of the universe by saying that order and understandability are natural to the universe, that the universe is simply like that. In other words, the nonbeliever cannot have his cake and eat it too. If explanations which appeal to the nature of a thing, which say that something has certain characteristics because that is the sort of thing it is are bad explanations when applied to God, then they are equally bad when applied to the universe. But nonbelievers sometimes reject this sort of explanation as applied to God, and then turn around and apply the same sort of explanation to the universe.

Why do some people reject explanations which appeal to the nature of a thing? Because, in their view, such explanations do not explain. If I ask why a certain drug puts people to sleep and I am told that it is because of the sleep-inducing nature of that drug, it would seem that instead of an explanation I have just been given a restatement of the facts. As opposed to this, a real explanation would tell me how certain chemical combinations of elements in the drug acted on certain parts of the body to cause sleep. But there is a difficulty about this notion of a "real explanation." Although perhaps we can explain the action of the drug in terms of chemical action and the chemical action in terms of the physics of particles at some stage, we will have to come to an end of *that* sort of explanation. There must be some ultimate fact or facts which cannot be explained in terms of anything more fundamental.

At this point we will either have to say that these ultimate facts have no explanation or regard them as in some way not in need of explanation. One way of expressing the idea that some fact is not in need of explanation is to say that it is the way it is "by nature" or "because that is the way things are."

The religious believer regards the existence and nature of God as ultimate facts not in need of explanation. Many nonbelievers agree that some set of facts must be regarded as ultimate and not in need of explanation, but argue that it is the existence and nature of the universe itself which are ultimate and not in need of explanation, not the existence and nature of God. A nonbeliever who takes this point of view is in agreement with the religious believer that *some* fact or facts must be regarded as ultimate and not in need of explanation; he simply disagrees on which set of facts—the existence and nature of God, or the existence and nature of the universe.

Someone could also regard the existence and nature of the universe as a fact which is in need of explanation but for which there *is* no satisfactory explanation. People who take this attitude are likely to use expressions such as "The universe *just happens* to exist," or "There is *no reason* why the universe exists; it just does." So we have three possible views: the one just mentioned, which we will call the "No Reason" view; the view that it is the universe itself which is ultimate and not in need of explanation, which we will call the "Universe Ultimate" view; and the view that it is the existence and nature of God which is the ultimate and not in need of explanation, which we will call the "God Ultimate" view. Obviously there is no scientific experiment or observation that will determine which of these three views is correct; that decision must be made before we can settle anything scientifically. But which of these views is correct will make a considerable difference as to whether we *can* settle anything scientifically.

If we accept the No Reason view, that the existence and nature of the universe are in need of explanation but cannot be explained, it would be hard to see how we could have much confidence in science. If there is no reason why the ultimate facts about the universe are as they are, then there is no reason why they should remain as they are and no reason why our apparent understanding of them should not be completely illusory. The No Reason view is basically a form of skepticism, which is incompatible with any confidence in science.

The view that we have called the Universe Ultimate view seems at first to avoid skepticism, for on this view the apparent order and rationality of the universe are natural to it; the universe is by nature the sort of universe which forms understandable patterns. But there is a difficulty about this which has been raised by some religious believers.

If, as the Universe Ultimate view states, there is no intelligent power behind the universe, then everything in the universe is the result of the nature of the universe itself. That includes our own minds and their thinking about the universe. But if the universe is purely material and has no intelligence or purpose, then our minds are the result of something that is without intelligence or purpose. However, if this is true, then what confidence can we have in the working of our minds? How can what does not have intelligence—a purely material universe—be expected to produce intelligence? Would we trust a computer somehow programmed by natural forces without intelligence?

The religious believer argues that confidence in our own reasoning powers, the confidence which makes science possible, can be justified only by the God Ultimate view. If the ultimate fact which explains everything else and does not itself stand in need of explanation is the existence of an intelligent Being, then our intelligence can be trusted, for it comes from intelligence.

The supporter of the Universe Ultimate view can reply to this argument in several ways. He can simply argue that whatever the origins of our intellectual powers they do work effectively, and that unintelligent forces can produce intelligence because they evidently have! But once the doubt about the trustworthiness of our intelligence has been raised, this does not seem satisfactory. For our intelligence might work well enough on practical matters and yet fatally deceive us about more general or theoretical matters. So the supporter of the Universe Ultimate view needs to give some grounds for his confidence in reason other than its practical success.

An answer to the question of how unintelligent forces can produce intelligence is given by some supporters of the Universe Ultimate view. This answer invokes the idea of evolution by natural selection. In a situation where there is competition for survival and variation in inherited characteristics, some organisms will inherit characteristics which give them an advantage in the struggle. This may be something as minor as a slightly longer reach or quicker reaction time or some major mutation in an important characteristic. Whatever it is, if it gives the organism an advantage over others in the struggle for food and mates, then the organism will survive to pass on that characteristic to the next generation. Thus, favorable mutations establish themselves in a population.

In the Universe Ultimate view, intelligence is such a favorable mutation, or a group of such favorable mutations. Because intelligence was advantageous in the struggle to survive and reproduce, it established itself as a characteristic of certain organisms, which were our ancestors. Thus, intelligence arose from the struggle for survival by the process of natural selection. If we regard the struggle for survival as a nonintelligent process, then we have a plausible explanation of how unintelligent forces can produce intelligence. Thus, supporters of the Universe Ultimate view who take this line seem to have an answer to the objection raised by supporters of the God Ultimate view.

However, it is not clear that this defense of the Universe Ultimate view is satisfactory. While practical cunning evidently has survival value, it is not clear that theoretical reasoning of the kind used in philosophy or science has such value, especially in the primitive conditions in which the natural selection process has immediate and direct application. Furthermore, the natural selection process is simply one of adaptation to the existing environment, not a process of improvement or progress in any general sense. If our question is "Can human intelligence give us a trustworthy picture of the universe?" we do not answer *that* question by showing (if we can show) that intelligence has a survival value at a particular stage of the development of species. Many characteristics which have high survival value at one stage of development become disadvantages at a later stage, and at any rate the question of whether intelligence has survival value is separate from the question of whether intelligence can give us a true picture of the universe and our place in it.

We can say at least that the attempted defense of the Universe Ultimate view by means of a natural selection explanation of the development of human intelligence is open to a number of questions and objections. To pursue this line of argument successfully we would have to explore such matters as the relation between theoretical and practical intelligence, the connection between truth and survival value, and so on. If we cannot answer these question satisfactorily we will have to concede considerable force to the claim of some religious believers that the religious view can give a reasonable account of the success of science, while a purely naturalistic view such as the Universe Ultimate view cannot.

At this stage some religious believers and some nonbelievers would be content to call a draw, to concede that *both* the Universe Ultimate *and* the God Ultimate views are reasonable interpretations of our total experience and that it would be reasonable to adopt *either* view. We can distinguish between the Strong Rational Believer, who believes that a religious view gives a *more* reasonable view of our total experience than a nonreligious view, and the Strong Rational Nonbeliever who holds that some version of the Universe Ultimate view gives a better explanation of our total experience than any religious view. But we can also distinguish the Weak Rational Believer and the Weak Rational Nonbeliever, who hold that religious and nonreligious theories give an *equally* good account of our total experience, and who then opt for belief or unbelief on some other grounds—personal preference, intuition, a "leap of faith."

The two weak views have considerable attraction for people in our culture, for they seem to support a tolerant "pluralistic" view that believers and unbelievers are both reasonable, and that neither religion nor irreligion is unjustified or irrational. At the same time the two weak rational views seem more defensible than any kind of irrationalistic view. To ignore the evidence in deciding for religion or irreligion is a course of action which would be hard to justify. But if the arguments for and against religion are equally balanced, there seems to be nothing wrong with a "take your choice" attitude.

We should beware, however, of taking any view simply because it avoids difficulties or is in tune with current attitudes. Until we have thoroughly investigated the pros and cons, we cannot be sure that one of the strong views is not justified. And if either of the strong views can be justified, then it *is* unreasonable to make a personal decision as if the arguments were equally balanced.

Part of what we will be doing in the rest of this book is examining the pros and cons of religious belief and unbelief, as well as coming to a better understanding of what religious belief is. We will pay most of our attention to the kind of religious belief which has been most influential in the Western world—belief in a just and loving God who is the all-powerful and all-knowing Creator of the universe, and who rewards or punishes His creatures in a life after death. Toward the end of the book we will take a brief look at some non-Western views of religion. But until we come to our discussion of non-Western religions we will take religious belief as belief in God and in a life after death. Historically this describes the central core of belief in the two major Western religions,

Judaism and Christianity, and in the Near Eastern religion which most resembles them, Islam.

Sometimes "faith" is *contrasted* with belief as being somehow a "leap in the dark," a blind commitment to something we have no understanding of. But it is hard to see how this can be reconciled with the traditional view of religious belief or indeed with any reasonable view. For a complete leap in the dark might just as well be in any direction: toward Communism or belief in magic and witchcraft rather than toward religious belief. It seems both more reasonable and more in line with the traditional view of faith to say that faith is a special *kind* of belief, and the best way to understand faith is to first understand the nature of belief. The weakest sort of belief is what we may call "*mere* belief." When we are asked a question we sometimes give an answer in a qualified way, not claiming to know or even to be sure of our answer. By saying "I believe," we emphasize that we *merely* believe—we don't *know*. We also use "I think" for this sense of belief. In this sense of "belief" we would be surprised but not dumbfounded to find that we were wrong. We are not absolutely certain, and we are not giving our authority for what we say. Belief in this sense has little to do with religious faith.

Belief, in the stronger sense, where we are confident in what we believe and would be astounded if we were wrong, seems to have three major characteristics: 1) We must have some understanding of what we claim to believe; 2) We must be prepared to take action appropriate to our stated belief; and 3) We must have some reason for our belief.

Religious faith plainly shares these characteristics of belief in the strong sense. We might very well challenge a claim that a child had faith in some doctrine on the grounds that the child was too young to understand it. We often use the connection between faith and action to judge the faith of others: Martyrs, for example, are pre-eminently witnesses to their faith because only persons who really believe would act as they act. Finally, the idea that faith must be based on good reasons would seem to correspond with what would be said by most believers. A Jew might cite God's dealings with His people, a Christian the Resurrection of Christ; some Protestants would cite the authority of the Bible, some Catholics the authority of the Church. But it seems unlikely that most religious believers would be willing to say that they have no good reason at all for their belief, that they have simply taken a leap into total darkness. The *kind* of reasons cited may be quite different from reasons for other beliefs; what I am denying is that most believers would say that they had *no* good reasons for belief.

How, then, is faith *different* from belief in the strong sense? The differences seem to lie in 1) the kind of confidence involved; 2) the degree of understanding expected; 3) the kind of action we are committed to, and 4) the kinds of reasons we have for our belief.

The kind of confidence is different in that faith is generally regarded as more unshakable than belief, and also as more personal. Faith involves trust in a person, not just confidence in the truth of a statement, as when we speak of a child's faith in its father and mother. Religious faith in God: not only belief in His existence and in what He has revealed to man, but also *trust* in Him. Faith is also usually regarded as on a special level of certainty: one good dictionary defines faith as "unquestioning belief."

Faith also differs from mere belief in that we are usually willing to grant that we only partially understand the object of our faith. God is by definition infinitely greater than we are, and thus only partly comprehensible to us. His revelation to us might be full of things which we do not fully understand. Of course if we understood *nothing* of what we believe, our belief would be empty; but *partial* understanding is what we should expect in the nature of the case.

The third distinctive feature of faith is the nature of our commitment to it. We may strongly believe certain statements without being willing to suffer or die for them. But when a man suffers or dies for an idea or ideal, be it God, Reason, Democracy or Communism, we speak of his *faith* in God, in Reason, in Democracy, in Communism. A man who has nothing for which he will die or suffer may have opinions or beliefs, but he has no faith in anything.

Finally, faith is distinguished from both belief and knowledge by the sort of reasons we have for it. If we know something by experience or have a conclusive deductive argument for it, we say that we *know*, not that we have belief *or* faith. Thus, evidence of sufficient strength rules out faith. But if we *merely* have a probability, a gambler's chance, of being right, we do not speak of having faith either. Still, it is not just a matter of a degree of confidence exactly in between knowledge and probability. A man who has faith does not say, "I know," but he does not say, "I am ninety-nine percent certain," any more than he says, "I am eighty percent certain." But when asked for the evidence for a faith, there is a certain difficulty. For in a sense, the evidence for a faith is everything the man knows. He may indeed cite particular pieces of evidence. But the religious believer basically accepts his belief because it makes sense out of everything else he knows. And this is true also of the materialist, the Communist, and so on.

All "world-views" or "fundamental faiths" have this characteristic: they "make sense of things" for those who accept them. But unless we are to accept pure relativism, one of these views must be true and the others false. At most, one can *really* make sense of things, others must only appear to. To accept pure relativism is not to accept any world-view at all, for if a view is no more true than any other view, it explains nothing at all.

In the next chapter we will consider a major objection to religious beliefs, the existence of moral evil, and suffering. In later chapters we will consider arguments for the existence of God, including the question of whether miracles can be evidence for religious belief. Having considered these general topics we can then look at some more specific kinds of religious belief—the relation of Christianity and Judaism to their history and their holy books, the relevance of mystical experience, the contrast between Western and non-Western religions, and questions about life after death.

It is not my intention to convince you of the truth of any particular view of religion, but rather to increase your understanding of religious views so that you may have a better chance of making an intelligent judgment. To paraphrase Joanna's words to her daughter, if I do my job of teaching properly you will be able to make an intelligent decision of your own.

DISCUSSION QUESTIONS

1. Do you think that religious belief is a matter of personal decision? What do you mean by "personal decision"? If you think that religious belief is a matter of personal decision, what are your reasons? If you think it is not, what are your reasons?
2. Compare another method of settling disputes with the scientific method. What are the differences and similarities? Do both methods apply to the same subject matter?
3. What scientific discoveries seem to you to create difficulties for religious belief? Why?
4. How much disorder and incomprehensibility in the universe would there have to be before we gave up trying to give scientific explanations? Could there be a scientific explanation of a *totally* chaotic situation? Why or why not?
5. What difficulties can you see in the idea of explaining the characteristics of something by saying that it has a certain nature? What difficulties can you see if we do not explain anything in this way?
6. What would be the effect on science if we regarded the ultimate facts about the universe as in need of explanation but impossible to explain? Support your answer.
7. Can we consistently hold both that our thoughts are the result of

mindless forces *and* that our thinking gives us reliable information about the universe? Why or why not?

8.   Does the God Ultimate view assume any characteristics in God besides intelligence? If so, what characteristics and why? If not, why not?

9.   Try to give a stronger version of the argument that natural selection explains our confidence in our reasoning powers. What difficulties do you see in your strengthened version?

10.   Would you classify your own position as you begin this book as strong theism, weak theism, strong nontheism, or weak nontheism? Why do you hold this view? Would your reasons convince another person?

SUGGESTED READINGS

BRODY, BARUCH A., Ed., *Readings in the Philosophy of Religion.* Englewood Cliffs, N.J.: Prentice-Hall Inc., 1974:
   FLEW, ANTONY, HARE, RICHARD, and MITCHELL, BASIL, "The University Discussion," pp. 308–315.
   HICK, JOHN, "Theology and Verifications," pp. 315–330.
HICK, JOHN H., *Philosophy of Religion.* 2d ed. Englewood Cliffs, N.J.: Prentice-Hall Inc., 1973:
   Introduction and Chapter 1, pp. 1–15.
   Chapter 6, pp. 84–96.
YANDELL, KEITH, Ed., *God, Man and Religion.* New York: McGraw-Hill Book Company, 1973:
   PATON, H. J., "Intellectual Impediments to Religious Belief," pp. 117–75.
   ALSTON, WILLIAM P., "Psychological Explanation of Religious Belief," pp. 122–46.

The Problem of Evil:

"How Could God Permit That?"

2

Detective-Lieutenant Corrigan pushed open the fire door and stepped out onto the fire escape. He unpinned the badge from his lapel, since he was leaving the crime scene, and fumbled for a cigarette. The tall man in the windbreaker, which was opened to to reveal a Roman collar, turned from where he had been leaning on the railing and nodded. "Pretty bad in there, Father," said Corrigan with an edge in his voice.

"I imagine we've both seen worse," replied the priest, his face tired and strained, "but it was bad."

Corrigan started to speak, hesitated, and then burst out, "How can you believe in God when you see things like that? How could God permit that kind of thing if there was a God? The guy maybe brought it on himself, taking that junk, and the woman at least chose to live with him knowing he was on the stuff. But those poor kids . . ."

The priest shuddered a little, remembering the hysterical screaming of the two children who had survived and the sprawled, bloody bodies of the two that hadn't. "I know what you mean, Lieutenant" he said, "but it's believing in God that makes me able to face things like that. Knowing that the ones

who died are with God, and that the pain the others have suffered isn't useless."

Corrigan rubbed the back of his neck with the hand that
wasn't holding his cigarette, an unconscious gesture he used
when trying to think out a problem. "Yeah, the dead ones I can
see; if you really believe in something after death I guess people dying isn't such a big deal. And maybe these two will at
least be scared off of drugs for the rest of their lives, even if they
have nightmares for a while. But you know as well as I do that
plenty of kids, and grown-ups too, in this neighborhood do plenty
of suffering that's no use to them or anyone else."

The priest shook his head. "No use we can see, maybe" he
replied, "but that any suffering is no use at all is just what I
don't accept. If you do think that there's wasted, useless suffering I can see why you question whether there's a God. I
couldn't believe in a God who lets people suffer for no reason."

Corrigan scowled, "I can't accuse you of leading a sheltered
life, I guess. I know you guys at Saint Dominic's see about as
much of the dirty side of this neighborhood as we do. But if you
think that there's any reason that could be good enough for
all the lousy things that go on . . ."

The priest cut in. "There's only one reason good enough,
really. That all men should be saved and come to the knowledge
of God. Some of us suffer for our own salvation, some of us suffer
for the salvation of others."

There was almost a sneer in the burly detective's voice as
he said, "Pretty hard on those who have to suffer for the others,
isn't it?"

"Hardest of all on One," replied the priest.

Corrigan didn't understand at first, then said a little uncertainly, "Oh, you mean—Him. Yeah, but why create a mess and
then get yourself crucified to clean it up?"

The priest's reply was dry. "The way I heard the story, we
made the mess."

Corrigan shook his head as if to clear it. "Do people still
believe in all that Adam and Eve stuff? You're an educated man,
Father—you know about evolution."

The other man grinned. "Since I've taught biology, among
other subjects, I may even know a bit more than you do, Lieutenant. There's actually nothing biologically absurd about the
idea of the human race descending from a single pair. Human
intelligence is quite plausibly to be considered a major mutation

—a big jump in evolution. But all the church actually requires us to believe about the "Fall of Man" is that the human race right at the beginning in some way refused obedience to God, as we've certainly been doing ever since, and this created the separation between man and God, which is the reason for all our problems."

The detective grunted, "I'd have thought our problems had lots of reason. Sex, money, drugs, violence . . ."

The priest nodded. "Yes, but all those came down to man trying to be a God to himself. Trying to impose his will on others, ignoring his limitations, trying to find happiness where it can't be found."

Corrigan stubbed out his cigarette. "Got to get back to work, Father. I guess what you're saying makes sense—for you. Maybe it's the cop in me but if I had the power I'd keep people from doing the things to each other that they do. Maybe it'll all work out in the end—I suppose we've got to hope so. Meantime we've got to clean up the messes."

The priest zipped up his windbreaker. "Yes, I've got work to do too. Maybe it's the priest in me, but I don't find that keeping people from doing things really solves problems in the long run. It's their hearts you've got to change. And I don't know any way of changing hearts but prayer—and suffering."

The detective held open the fire door for him to pass through. "Well, Father," he said, "say one for me—I've kind of got out of the habit since I came to this precinct."

Most of us lead fairly sheltered lives with respect to both suffering and moral evil. We are not likely to know a major criminal or see a major crime, and if a friend or relative has a severe accident or illness, he or she is likely to be hidden away in a hospital, where his or her suffering is out of our sight if not out of our minds. Thus our first experience of real moral evil or severe suffering is sometimes shattering. But such experiences seem to push people toward religious belief as often as they push them away from it, and religious believers as a group certainly are as familiar with sin and suffering as are nonbelievers.

Most people would agree that the existence of suffering and evil in the world is a challenge to religious belief. But what sort of challenge, and how strong a challenge? To get this clear, let us consider three possible claims that might be made about the way in which the existence of evil and suffering should affect our belief in God:

Claim I. If a good, all-powerful God existed, He would not permit any suffering or moral evil at all. Since suffering and moral evil obviously do exist, such a God does not exist.

This claim breaks down into two parts: that a good God would not permit suffering, and that a good God would not permit moral evil. Since most religious believers think of Heaven as a place without moral evil and without suffering, we might put this more picturesquely by saying that Claim I is the claim that a good God would create only a Heaven, and would not create a world such as the one we see around us.

The first answer a religious believer might give to this claim would begin with a distinction. If God had created a world of creatures without freedom of choice, with no free will, moral evil would of course have been impossible. And a world without the possibility of moral evil might well be a world without suffering, since suffering would seem to serve no purpose in such a world. But, the religious believer might claim, if you have a world containing persons with genuine freedom of choice, then suffering is a necessary element of such a world, for only by suffering can persons develop character.

This seems to be true in a very basic way. For if we never had unpleasant experiences—if everything occurred just as we wanted it, or if we liked everything that occurred—then it would be hard to see how we could even realize ourselves as persons distinct from other persons and from our environment. If a baby received everything it wanted as soon as it formed the wish, then it would think of persons and things outside itself as mere extensions of its own personality, like its fingers and toes. But if we do not get what we want or do not like what we get, we suffer—that, basically, is what suffering is.

So if other persons did precisely what we wanted or if we were always pleased with what they did, we would not recognize them as distinct persons. But beyond this, it is when we first begin to realize that other persons can be hurt just as we can, that we really see them as persons. A toy or doll or machine cannot be hurt, and we need not consider its feelings. But persons are not toys or dolls or machines, and it is when we begin to realize this that we begin to develop morally. Some of the most horrifying crimes have been committed by "moral solipsists"—people who do not seem to realize that there are other persons besides themselves, who treat other persons as things. Without the realization of pain in ourselves and in other persons, we would all be solipsists. Moral growth begins when we realize "This action hurts that other person. *I* wouldn't like to be hurt; he doesn't either."

There are several replies that could be made at this stage of the argument. The supporters of Claim I might try to argue that we do not have free choice and therefore, even if pain and suffering were a means of moral development in free persons, this does not justify *our* pain and suffering. The issue of free will is a complex one, and for the moment we will merely say that religious believers who use the kind of reply to Claim I discussed above are taking it for granted that we do have free choice and that most other people also take this for granted. They may be wrong, but arguments would be needed to show this.

A second objection which could be raised to the religious believers' reply to Claim I is the fact of animal suffering. Animals do not seem to have moral choice, and therefore cannot commit moral evil. But they do suffer physical pain, and this cannot be explained as necessary for their moral development since they do not have moral characters. This is a difficult objection to answer, if only because we have no inside knowledge of what animals feel. It is clear, however, that pain serves a biological purpose in enabling animals to survive, and that an animal that felt no pain would not avoid damage or death very long. The religious believer may agree that if God had created the world only for the sake of animals, it might have been a world without death and damage and perhaps therefore without pain. But if one of the reasons for the creation of this world was the moral development of persons, then it must be a world with danger and suffering. How animal suffering fits into the whole picture we may not completely understand, but if we can find a satisfactory solution to the problem of human suffering, we may have confidence that there is also a solution to the problem of suffering in animals.

We have seen at least a plausible answer to the question as to why a good God would allow some suffering: because without it the development of character is impossible. While of course more could be said about the questions raised so far, let us now consider a second claim, which could be put forward even by those who might grant what we have said up to this point.

Claim II. Even granted that there is a reason for permitting some moral evil and some suffering, if a good God existed, He would not allow the *amount* of moral evil and suffering which does in fact exist. Therefore a good God does not exist.

This is a much more difficult claim to deal with because it involves matters of amount and proportion. If it is granted that a good God could allow *some* evil and suffering, then where can a line be drawn? How much evil and suffering is too much for a good God to allow? And how much would not be too much? Half as much as actually exists? A tenth? A hundredth?

An important point to consider is the relation between permitting moral evil and permitting pain and suffering. If God allows human beings to make choices which are genuinely free, and some of those choices are morally wrong choices, what will be the result? Given that there are possibilities of causing pain and suffering to others and that some people by wrong moral choices exploit those possibilities for their own ends, then what could God do without taking away human freedom? If God steps in to nullify the bad results of the use of human freedom, how will people learn not to make wrong moral choices?

The difficulty, of course, is that wrong moral choices often hurt the innocent rather than the guilty. Most of us would have far fewer difficulties about the amount of pain and suffering in the world if suffering were always proportionate to wrongdoing: if no innocent person ever suffered and if each evildoer suffered in exact proportion to his sins. But innocent people do suffer and people seem to suffer out of all proportion for relatively minor failings. A few minutes of careless driving can lead to untold anguish for the driver and for innocent people he may involve in an accident.

At least a partial answer can be given to this difficulty by seeing that we often realize the wrongness of our moral choices only when these choices do cause suffering to innocent people. Someone who is relatively powerless to harm others—a child, for example—may have selfish or destructive attitudes which, because of his powerlessness, do no harm, but which are destroying the person's capacity for love and appreciation of things outside himself. It can happen that if people do manage to do some harm to others, and see the effect of their selfishness and hatred, this brings them at last to a realization of what they have become.

All very well, it might be replied, for the person who realizes and perhaps repents and reforms. But the innocent people are still injured, through no fault of their own. This objection brings us to our third and final claim, which might be put in this way:

Claim III. Setting aside the total amount of suffering, a good God will not cause or allow innocent persons to suffer for the sins of others. Since innocent people do suffer for the sins of others, a good, all-powerful God does not exist.

This claim is an attempt to detour around the question of how *much* suffering might be justified and to claim that certain *kinds* of suffering, which do seem to occur, are incompatible with the existence of a God in the traditional sense—both all good and all-powerful. Certainly some human beings—at least very young children—seem to be without any personal guilt of any kind. And some of these innocent human beings do seem to suffer more than could possibly be needed for the formation of their own character.

Different religious traditions have different answers to this problem and we will see, in our chapter on Eastern religions, an answer given in the Buddhist and Hindu traditions. But in this chapter I will discuss some answers to this problem which are part of the Christian religious tradition, since this is the one which is most likely to have affected, either positively or negatively, most people who will be reading this.

The two answers to the problem of suffering to be discussed are first, the doctrine of *original sin,* and second, the doctrine of *vicarious atonement.* Since these are theological doctrines, which are supposed to be known by revelation from God and not by argument, philosophy cannot directly decide the question of their truth or falsity. But we can consider the philosophical question as to whether these doctrines make sense and whether, *if* true, they would solve the problem of the suffering of innocent persons. Insofar as religious believers are merely defending their views against attack or answering a challenge, it is enough for them to show that their views are understandable and that they do meet the challenge. Of course repelling an attack is merely avoiding defeat; if the religious believer wants to convince anyone that his answers are true and should be accepted, different kinds of argument will be needed. But for the moment we are merely concerned to answer the nonbeliever's objections.

The notion of *original sin* in Christian theology is based, at least in part, on the story in the Book of Genesis which is part of the Jewish Torah as well as of the Christian Old Testament. But most Jews would reject this doctrine, at least in the form which Christian theology has given it, so we will talk only of the Christian version of the doctrine. Within Christianity there is a wide variety of interpretations of the idea of original sin, and it will be helpful to separate the historical question from the ethical question involved. The historical question is that of how literally we are to take the Adam and Eve story in Genesis, while the ethical question is the justifiability of letting someone here and now suffer for something done at an earlier time by other persons, even if those persons were the ancestors of those who now suffer.

In our introductory story I pictured the priest as making two points about the historical question—first, that there is no scientific impossibility in the origin of the human race from a single couple, and secondly, that the essentials of the doctrine of original sin are that the human race as a whole has in some way from the beginning refused obedience to God, thereby creating a separation from God which is the source of such things as war, disease, etc. that cause suffering to innocent persons.

This is a very general and cautious statement of the doctrine, but Christians in a good many denominations and traditions would agree that the doctrine means *at least* this. At any rate, this statement is enough to enable us to raise the ethical question, which is the question of collective guilt, or collective responsibility. Are we to regard human beings as properly responsible only for their own actions and mistakes, or is there a sense in which, *as* human beings, they can share a collective responsibility and even a collective guilt?

When we discuss this question in the context of such present-day problems as white guilt for past injustices to black persons, similar questions come up. Because I am a descendant of racial groups who have exploited and enslaved other groups, do I have some responsibility for reparation to those groups? In cases like this it helps to see that I have inherited many advantages from my ancestors so that it is only fair that I should inherit their liabilities, just as someone who inherits a family business must expect to inherit its debts as well as the stock and the good will.

Can we apply this analogy to the human race as a whole? Can we say that in inheriting life itself as well as the many advantages of centuries of human civilization, we must also accept some responsibility for the sins and errors of our ancestors? Perhaps so. But the difficulty seems to be that some of us seem to get mainly the advantages and some of us mainly the disadvantages. If suffering were evenly distributed over all people who were personally innocent, we might be willing to grant that they were bearing their part in the responsibilities inherited from past generations. But suffering is not equally distributed: of two innocent persons, one seems to suffer out of all proportion, the other hardly at all. The moral equation still does not seem to balance, even if we accept some responsibility of later generations for the morally wrong choices of earlier ones.

And, of course, at least some people would dig in their heels at this point, refusing to admit there is any justice in "inherited" responsibilities. The question really is how we should regard the human race: as a number of unconnected units not owing anything to one another, or as a sort of organic unity in which both benefits and responsibilities are shared.

To give the full answer of traditional Christianity to the problem of the apparently unjust distribution of suffering, we must go on to discuss the second doctrine, that of *vicarious atonement*. According to this doctrine the suffering of one person can benefit others; specifically, one person's suffering can make up for the wrong moral choices of another. For the Christian, the suffering and death of Christ was "for our sins," and his suffering and death somehow earned a new chance for the human race, so that through Christ's actions we can again be united to God. Some Christians would go on to say that by their sufferings, those who are personally innocent of moral evil can somehow unite themselves with the sufferings of Christ and that by their suffering they do what is within their power to make up for the sins of others and to help reunite the human race to God.

Two major objections are made to this doctrine by nonbelievers. The first is that the doctrine is nonsensical, and the second is that even if it makes sense it is immoral. The objection that the doctrine doesn't make sense can be put in the following way: "My morally wrong choices are my own responsiblity. Perhaps if *I* am punished for my wrong moral choices I will be sorry for what I have done, but at any rate I have brought the punishment on myself. But how can there ever be any connection between my wrongdoing and the sufferings of Christ or the suffering of some other innocent person who may be completely unknown to me? To say that the suffering of that person makes up for my wrongdoing makes no sense."

There are three different levels on which a religious believer might attempt to answer this objection. On the first level, he can point out that if a punishment is merely nullified, with no one paying for wrongdoing, we are inclined to treat the offense lightly and do the same thing again. If we are punished ourselves, resentment and anger may get in the way of repentance. But if someone else generously takes on the consequences of our wrongdoing, then our realization of and appreciation of the other person's self-sacrifice can provide a very powerful motive for repentance, if the least spark of love or gratitude remains in us.

On an even deeper level, it can be pointed out that what some have called the *law of exchange* is fundamental to human experience. Human beings can help one another physically, literally bearing one another's burdens. They can help one another mentally by teaching or counseling one another. In these cases the help is most effective when we literally or in an extended sense take the place of the other person. If I lift the bundle from your shoulders, then you are no longer carrying it. The best teacher is the one who can put himself in the student's place and appreciate the problem from the student's point of view; the best counselor is the one who can appreciate the feelings and desires of the person he is trying to help.

There is a long Christian tradition which says that we can also help others by putting ourselves in their place in another sense and bearing the suffering that is the consequence of their actions. Sydney Carton, in *A Tale of Two Cities*, takes the place of another man in the condemned cell; many friends, or husbands or wives or parents or children have given up their lives for their loved ones or taken on their sufferings. Christians remember the words of Christ about taking up their cross and following Him, and the saying that "greater love has no man than that he lay down his life for his friend."

At this stage the moral objection may be raised: It is not *fair*, it may be said, to let one person suffer for another. Each person should take the consequences of his own wrongdoing: No one should be asked or allowed to bear the sufferings deserved by another. There are two cases to consider here: one, the case of a volunteer, the other, the case of someone who has not consciously chosen to suffer for others. To forbid, on moral grounds, that one person should voluntarily take on the burdens of another seems very strange. To most human beings self-sacrificing love has seemed the best and noblest thing in human experience: Not to allow us to suffer for those we love would be to rob love of what seems to many to be its highest expression.

But what about those who have not deliberately chosen to suffer for others? Accepting a voluntary sacrifice is one thing; demanding an involuntary sacrifice is surely another. Here again we must distinguish two possibilities. Some people who suffer for others without deliberately choosing to are glad when they realize what they have accomplished for the other person. If they had been asked and if they had fully realized what was involved, they would gladly have volunteered. Some people, however, even if they had been asked to make a sacrifice for others and even if they had realized the good they could have done for them, might still have refused. And since suffering for others to whom we have no obligation is above and beyond the call of duty, we cannot say that the refusal is morally wrong.

However, in the Christian view, what God has in mind for all of us human beings is that we should love one another as Christ loved us— that is, love one another enough to suffer and die for one another. In this view the purpose of human beings is to form a community of love, what St. Paul called the mystical body of Christ. Each member of this community will be glad to have helped the other members, to have suffered for them if necessary. Thus all those who become part of this community of love will be either explicitly or implicitly volunteers, glad either in advance or in retrospect to sacrifice themselves for others. Thus the suffering of the innocent is not wasted and is not an imposition on them. In the long run persons of good will who have suffered will be glad that they have suffered—glad for their own sake, or glad for the sake of others.

What about the suffering of those who are not persons of good will, who hate and reject others? Some of it, in the Christian view, will be deserved, will be simply what they have brought on themselves. Some of it, Christians will hope, may be part of a process that will lead to repentance and reform. But does any person suffer for the sake of others who has not deserved that suffering and who will not in the long run be glad of that suffering? The answer most Christians would give is no. Suffering for others is a privilege, a share in Christ's work. Those who have no share in Christ have no share in His work.

If these Christian doctrines are true, then they may offer a solution to the problem of apparently undeserved suffering in this world. But some Christians at least still hold that it is possible, by misuse of our free will, to separate ourselves from God forever—to condemn ourselves to eternal separation from all that is good and so to eternal suffering. The moral question raised by unbelievers, which also troubles many Christians, is "How could a good God permit anyone to suffer eternally?" Surely no puny action of ours could *deserve* such punishment, and no benefit to others could arise from such punishment.

Christians have been divided on this issue. Some great representatives of the Christian tradition have dared to hope that since St. Paul tells us that God "desires all men to be saved and to come to the knowledge of God," His will will not in the long run be frustrated by our rebellions. They have hoped that after a process, perhaps very long and very painful, even the worst of human beings will choose to accept the offer of love in God.

However, here the issue of freedom is crucial. If freedom is really genuine, then it must include the possibility of choosing evil and rejecting good. Our own unhappy experience shows us that we sometimes reject joy and peace simply because we stubbornly insist on our own way. God wants all men to freely choose Him, but if we are genuinely free, then may some men not choose to reject God? And if they freely so choose and persist in this refusal, then what can be the result but eternal separation from the good?

An intermediate position between Universalism—the belief that all persons will someday be united with God—and the traditional belief that at least some persons are eternally punished, is the view that separation from God will eventually lead to nonexistence: that in rejecting God we reject all goods including the good of existence, which also comes from God, and that the person who rejects God eventually passes out of existence. Some Christians would support this idea on Biblical grounds; fire, which is used as the symbol of Hell's sufferings not only hurts but eventually destroys. Some may never accept God, but if so they will not always exist to reject God.

Many Christians, however, cannot reconcile this interpretation with God's revelation as they understand it, and conclude that some who reject God will be allowed to exist and maintain their rejection eternally. What the state of those persons will be is perhaps unimaginable to us; the important thing is that we could be like them. They have rejected God of their own free will and God has merely followed through His gift of free will by not forcing them to accept Him. We too have free will, and we too could so abuse it as to reject everything outside ourselves and be left to ourselves eternally. Thus some Christians see the idea of eternal punishment as the inescapable corollary of free will.

The nonbeliever's final objection might center on this point. Granted that the price of free will is this high; why should God have created creatures with free will? Many religious believers, Christian and non-Christian, would reply that anything good brings with it corresponding dangers. A plant cannot suffer but equally cannot feel enjoyment. An animal cannot worry about the future but equally cannot hope for or anticipate the future. Beings without free will could not reject God but equally could not accept God of their own choice. These religious believers hold that likeness to God consists in being able to know *and* to choose. Our knowledge is incomplete but is nevertheless real knowledge, and our choices, however imperfect, are genuine choices. God allows us to make our choices; He does not make them for us or force us to make them.

To the determinist the whole idea of individual choice seems mistaken. In a determinist view every event has *determining* causes; for every event B there is a previous event A such that when A occurred B was bound to occur. This is quite distinct from the more modest view that every event has *enabling* causes: that for any event B, there must be some previous event A which *enabled* B to happen; if A *had not* occurred, *B could not have* occurred. Even this view may be too broad, since it seems to lead to an infinite regress of causes. But at any rate, all of the events we experience certainly have enabling causes, including our own choices. If I had not been born, had not learned English, etc., I could not have chosen to write these words.

The most important single thing to notice about the arguments for determinism is that almost all such arguments from science or experience confuse enabling causes and determining causes. From the obvious fact that all events in our experience have enabling causes it is concluded, illegitimately, that all events have determining causes. There are also purely logical arguments for determinism, but when carefully examined, all such arguments turn out to assume what they are attempting to prove. There are also theological arguments for determinism, and we will examine some of these in a later chapter. But for the moment the situation can be summed up as follows: There are no conclusive arguments against the idea that human beings have free will, which is to say that some human choices have no determining causes. If God has given us free will we can see that *some* moral evil must be possible, and that at least some pain and suffering will be necessary to form our moral character. If moral evil causes suffering and if God cannot remove the suffering without frustrating its operation in forming moral character, then the amount of suffering in the world does not seem a conclusive argument against the existence of a good God. The suffering of innocent persons seems the hardest problem to solve, but granted the Christian idea that God wants to form us into a community of self-sacrificing love, we can see the part that suffering might play. The notion of eternal suffering poses a final problem, but perhaps the possibility of final rejection of God is an inescapable consequence of free will.

If these arguments are successful, then the religious believer has shown that the existence of moral evil and suffering does not provide an argument against religious belief. In the following chapters we will consider whether there are any successful arguments for religious belief. If there are not, the situation is a standoff, and neither the believer nor the unbeliever can claim victory. But if there are good arguments for religious belief, then the failure of objections based on moral evil and suffering would be a step in showing that religious belief is *more* rational than nonbelief.

Surprisingly enough, the argument from evil is the only major argument which has been advanced against the existence of God, in the sense of being an attempt to *disprove* His existence. There have been a number of attempts to explain away belief in God on psychological or sociological grounds, but we can see, by briefly considering several points, that such explanations do not *disprove* God's existence.

The first point is that merely offering an alternative explanation does not disprove any theory or idea. First an alternative theory must be shown to be coherent and to fit the known facts. Once this has been done we are faced with two *possible* explanations. We can reasonably reject the established theory in favor of a new theory only if the new theory can be shown to be *superior* on some grounds to the established theory.

The second point is that in general the question of the origin of our beliefs is logically irrelevant to the truth or falsity of those beliefs. The appeal to the alleged origins of our beliefs as a substitute for arguments pro or con about the beliefs themselves is called by logicians the *genetic fallacy*, and is condemned in most elementary logic books.

The final point is that plausible explanations of ideas in terms of their psychological origins can almost always be given on both sides of an argument, and tend to cancel each other out.

The force of these last two points is that even if psychology or sociology were able to give a completely plausible explanation of the origin of our religious beliefs in psychological terms, this would not settle the question of the truth or falsity of those beliefs. Unless we begin with a prejudgment that a belief is false and a predisposition to accept any other possible explanation, psychological or sociological explanations of our beliefs carry little weight.

Thus, even if such an explanation of religious belief were completely satisfactory, it would not show that it was unreasonable to believe in God; no doubt psychological and sociological explanations could be given for many true beliefs. But in fact most psychological and sociological explanations of religious belief are open to many criticisms. One general criticism of such explanations is this: Are the psychological or sociological theories by which religion is to be explained away exempt from the sort of criticism they apply to other theories? If not, they can themselves be explained away. But if they claim exemption for themselves, on what grounds do they do so? If any theory can still be true despite psychological or sociological explanations of why it is held, then why cannot religious beliefs still be true despite psychological or sociological explanations of why *they* are held?

One final argument against belief in God which we will take a brief look at is the claim that the idea of God is somehow self-contradictory or nonsensical. There are two forms of this claim. The first is that some of the traditional attributes of God, such as omnipotence or omniscience, are contradictory in themselves; the second is that some of these attributes contradict one another or contradict other parts of traditional religious belief. Thus it is claimed that we cannot consistently accept the traditional idea of God.

Most such arguments seem to rest on logical quibbles which it would not be especially profitable to examine in detail in an introductory book. But to give some idea of what those arguments are like, I will briefly examine one alleged inconsistency of each kind. It has sometimes been claimed, for instance, that the traditional idea of omnipotence is self-contradictory, for if God "can do anything" this will create paradoxes. Could God, for example, create a square circle, create a stone that even He could not lift, or do something which He does not do? If He cannot, then there is something He cannot do, while if it is alleged that God could do these things, we seem to be talking nonsense.

All that is necessary to clear up these alleged paradoxes is to understand clearly what is meant by saying that God is "omnipotent" or "all-powerful." It does not mean that God can do things which are self-contradictory in themselves, contradictory to His own existence, or contradictory to His doing them. Thus, a square circle is contradictory in itself, since nothing can both have straight sides and corners and at the same time be circular. A stone which cannot be lifted is inconsistent with the existence of an all-powerful being, just as an immovable object is inconsistent with the existence of an irresistible force. An immovable object could logically exist, but then there would be no irresistible force. An irresistible force could logically exist, but then there would be no immovable object. So an unliftable stone, though not *self*-contradictory, is inconsistent with the existence of an all-powerful being.

The question as to whether God can do what He does not do is even more complex. An action can be described in such a way that by definition God does not do it, either directly—"Let X be an action which God does not do"—or indirectly—"Let Y be the action of *me* scratching my head" (thereby making it true by definition that I perform the action and not God). In either case, of course, if we say "God does X" or "God does Y," given those definitions, we have a contradiction. Therefore, X and Y are not actions which God can bring about, since their being brought about by God involves a contradiction.

But this is perfectly harmless if, by saying that God is all-powerful or omnipotent we *mean* that God can bring about any state of affairs, S, such that S is 1) consistently describable, 2) not inconsistent with the existence of God, and 3) not inconsistent with God's bringing it about. And once these puzzles are brought to our attention we see that this is just what we do mean by God's being all-powerful or omnipotent. This involves no *real* limitation on the power of God, for God can still create any genuine shape, can still create and lift weights of any size, and still bring about any *kind* of event, such as my head's being scratched. All that God *cannot* do is create some shape corresponding to a contradictory description, bring about states of affairs inconsistent with His own existence, and do things and at the same time not do them. But none of these limitations on omnipotence have any religious significance at all.

Similar things might be said about most supposed incompatibilities between different attributes of God. For instance, God has traditionally been thought of as unchanging, since, being perfect, He cannot change either for the better or for the worse. Is this inconsistent with God's acting or doing things in a changing world, or being aware of what is going on in a changing world, as some philosophers have claimed? Again, if God's unchangeability is properly understood, there is no contradiction. What is thought of in religious terms as significant about God's unchangeability is that His *nature* does not change; He is always good, loving, forgiving, etc. But there seems no *religious* reason why God's *relation* to His creatures should not change: if I am farther from God, God is farther from me. The change is in me, not in God. Since these attributes of God which can be thought of as changing are all relational properties, this general principle can be used to solve a number of difficulties about "changes in God." The changes are not in Him, but in His relation to other things.

One difficulty which may be to some extent a genuine difficulty rather than just a logical puzzle, is the relationship between God's foreknowledge and human free will. Most religious believers think that God knows the future, but a great many of them hold that human actions are free (though some Calvinist Christians and some Moslems would disagree). Are those who hold both that God knows the future and that human beings are free holding inconsistent beliefs?

The detailed solution to this problem is highly complex, but the general lines of a solution can be given clearly enough. Either free actions are such that it is logically impossible for God to know them in advance, or they are not. If they are logically impossible to know in advance, then it is not a real limitation on God's knowledge that He cannot know them, any more than it is a real limitation on His power that He cannot create a square circle. If it is not logically impossible to know free actions in advance, then there is no problem; whether we can understand *how* He does it or not, God could know free actions in advance.

There still seems to be a religious difficulty if we are forced to say that God cannot know free actions in advance, for traditionally, God is thought of as knowing the future. But a religiously adequate form of the view that God knows the future can still be saved. If we can make sense of the idea that God is somehow "outside of time," then we can say that God does not *fore*know free actions, but simply *sees* them in an "eternal now" which is not the same as our temporal "now." But even if we cannot made adequate sense of this deep and difficult notion of God being out-side of time, it does not follow that we must deny that God knows the future. Since God is all-powerful and supremely wise, He can bring about any event He chooses, at any time He chooses, and thus, so to speak, "outmaneuver" human free will, just as a master chess player playing with a beginner can bring the game to any conclusion he likes.

We have said enough to see a pattern in the kind of objection based on the supposed inconsistency of the idea of God. The objector seizes on some religiously important attribute of God, and interprets it in such a way as to raise logical difficulties. But the logical difficulties are almost never of any religious importance, and it would seem that the religious believer can always interpret the attribute in question in such a way as to avoid the difficulty without losing anything of religious importance.

So far as we can see, then, none of the kinds of objection to the ex-istence of God which we have considered are barriers to accepting the existence of God. In the following chapters we will examine the question of whether there are any positive reasons for accepting the existence of God.

DISCUSSION QUESTIONS

1. In your own experience has suffering ever led to improvement in character? Could the improvement have taken place without the suf-fering?

2. Could persons develop character in a world without suffering?

Try to imagine a world where this could occur.

3. Suffering sometimes seems to cause worsening of character rather than improvement. How does this affect the argument about the relation of suffering to character development?

4. What problems does the suffering of animals pose for religious belief? What solution would you offer to the problem? If you think the problem has no solution, give your reasons.

5. Granting for the sake of argument that some amount of suffering can be justified, is there any amount of suffering that would be impossible to justify? How would one determine what amount of suffering could or could not be justified?

6. What *kinds* of suffering seem especially difficult to justify? Why?

7. What is your understanding of the doctrine of original sin? What objections do you have to this doctrine? If you have no objections to it, what answers would you give to some of the objections mentioned in this chapter?

8. What is your understanding of the doctrine of vicarious atonement? What objections do you have to this doctrine? If you have no objections, how would you answer the objections given in this chapter?

9. Would you agree that the suffering of innocent people is justified if it helps others and if in the long run the sufferers would be glad they have suffered? Why or why not?

10. What objections or additions do you have to what has been said in this chapter?

SUGGESTED READINGS

BRODY, BARUCH, A., ed., *Readings in the Philosophy of Religion*. Englewood Cliffs, N.J.: Prentice-Hall, Inc., 1974:
    HUME, DAVID, "The Argument from Evil," pp. 149–56.
    MACKIE, J. L., "Evil and Omnipotence," pp. 157–67.
    PLANTINGA, ALVIN, "The Free Will Defense," pp. 186–99.
    PIKE, NELSON, "Hume on Evil," pp. 200–213.
HICK, JOHN H., *Philosophy of Religion*. 2d ed., 1973. Englewood Cliffs, N.J.: Prentice-Hall, Inc., 1933.
    Chapter 3, "Grounds for Disbelief in God," pp. 36–42.
YANDELL, KEITH, ed., *God, Man and Religion*. New York: McGraw-Hill Book Company, 1973:
    HOITENGA, DEWEY, "Logic and the Problem of Evil," pp. 334–50.
    YANDELL, KEITH, "A Response to Hoitenga," pp. 351–65.

3 *Arguments for God:*

Reason to Believe?

Mrs. Dale tried to sneak a look at her watch without the others' noticing. Surely it was her imagination which told her that the air was getting bad in the elevator. Even if the whole building had fallen down around the elevator car where it lay at the bottom of the shaft there must be enough air trapped with them to last until they were rescued. If they were rescued, that is. That had definitely been an earthquake tremor which had shaken the elevator and snapped the cable. The safety brakes had worked after a fashion, but it was probably lucky that they had been near the bottom of the old building. Better try to keep them talking, even if it wasted air, she thought. Panic could be even worse than suffocation. But it was a curious discussion to be carrying on in a wrecked elevator—or perhaps not so curious if they all thought, as she did, that they might not get rescued in time.

"So we all believe in God," she said, picking up the thread of their discussion. "That's a little unusual these days, for a randomly selected group like ours." Did she sound pedantic? she wondered. Probably. Being first a teacher and then a social worker did that to you. She went on, "Perhaps it would help pass the time if we each tried to say why we believe in God."

This is either a parlor game, she thought, or a very pertinent discussion. How well would her own belief survive if she knew that there was not going to be a rescue? What was it really founded on?

Larrigan, the janitor, was an uncouth little gnome, but he was quick-witted. He played up with a little deliberate exaggeration: "Ah, you learn it in school. How did the whole universe get here if God didn't put it here? And why would things be going on in a way the scientists can learn about if it was all just chance? If there's laws there's got to be a lawgiver. You learn it in school," he concluded dogmatically.

"I too have learned something like that in school," said Mrs. Chernick. Her heavily accented English had almost a comic effect, but she was one of Mrs. Dale's clients and Mrs. Dale knew that she was probably the best educated person in the elevator car, with degrees from two prestigious European universities. Despite her accent and her shabby appearance she still had an air of authority, and the others listened respectfully as she went on. "But I have always been more impressed by the argument that once we really understand what the word God means, we will at once see that such a Being must exist. It is like mathematics, you see. Once you know the definition, you know the thing."

This seemed to leave the others a little stunned and no one else said anything, so Mrs. Dale found herself blundering into speech. "Both those reasons sound very abstract to me. They don't seem to have a great deal to do with our everyday lives. I think that the thing that keeps my belief in God alive is the experience I've had with a few extraordinarily brave and good people. Their goodness—and goodness in general—couldn't have just happened, couldn't just be an accident thrown up by a meaningless universe. And even the indignation we feel at cruelty and injustice points the same way. If we were just absurd fragments of a meaningless universe we wouldn't feel the outrage we do." Mrs. Dale felt she was babbling and turned to Mr. Gustafson, who was sitting on the floor cross-legged, as he sat at his shoemaker's bench in the little shop on the ground floor of the building. "What do you think, Mr. Gustafson?"

He smiled at her with his gentle, dreamy smile. She had never noticed before how intense the pale blue of his eyes was. "I see God in my prayers, dear lady," he said. "There is a time for speaking about God, but it is better to speak *to* God when things are as they are now."

Mrs. Dale knew then that he shared her fears about being rescued in time. But just then there was a banging noise on the top of the elevator and an authoritative voice yelling, "You people in there! We'll have you out shortly." The others were on their feet at once looking at the roof, even reaching up to it, as if that would help. But from the corner of her eye Mrs. Dale could see Mr. Gustafson still cross-legged on the floor, his eyes shut now, but his smiling lips moving slightly as if he were whispering thanks to a friend.

There are many reasons for belief in God. Some religious believers are convinced, like Mr. Larrigan in our story, from the existence and orderliness of the universe that it must have been made by God. Others, like Mrs. Dale, base their belief on moral experience. Like the argument based on the existence and orderliness of the universe, this is an argument which starts from experiences of the kind both believers and unbelievers have had. Still another kind of argument is based on experiences which religious believers claim to be unique; perhaps Mr. Gustafson's remark, "I meet God in my prayers," could be interpreted in this way. Finally, philosophers have often been fascinated by the idea of showing that God must exist simply from the idea or definition of God, though this sort of argument has probably never had much influence with ordinary people.

With the exception of the last argument, all of the arguments for the existence of God which have been developed by philosophers are more sophisticated versions of ideas which have occurred to many human beings at many times in history. The ideas of a creator, or at least an arranger of the Universe, of a Lawgiver or Source of morality, of a higher Being who manifests Himself in dreams or visions, are found in most human societies, and have seemed to many the best explanations of our experience in these areas.

Without going into the whole story of the historical development of these ideas we will make a survey of the major arguments for God's existence, and try to assess the strength of these arguments. We will begin with the attempts to show that God exists from the very definition or idea of God; the technical name for this sort of argument is the *ontological argument*. The first developed version of the argument was given in the early Middle Ages by Anselm, an Italian theologian who became Archbishop of Canterbury in England, but there is also a later argument of this kind developed by the French philosopher, René Descartes.

The first ontological argument which we will consider is simply St. Anselm's first ontological argument, which occurs in Chapter II of Anselm's book, the *Proslogion*. It can be presented in the following way:

Some things exist in reality and some things are thought of. This obviously gives us four possible combinations:

1. Thought of and existing in reality;
2. Thought of, but not existing in reality;
3. Not thought of, existing in reality;
4. Not thought of, not existing in reality.

Fairly obviously some things neither exist nor are thought of, although we cannot give an example of this class without thinking of it, thereby putting the thing in question in the second class listed. Things which exist but are not thought of also cannot be discussed without thinking of them and so putting them in the first class listed, but there are obviously things of this sort—e.g., small bits of matter in remote corners of the universe. Things which are thought of but do not exist are legion— for example, my sailboat (which I have thought of owning but do not own and may never own). Things which exist and which are thought of obviously exist—for example I myself, the page you are reading, the sun, and so on.

Now consider God, whom Anselm defined as "the Being such that no greater being is possible." Such a Being is thought of, which means that He does not belong to class 3 or 4. But He cannot belong to class 2, for if God was thought of but did not exist, a greater being would be possible, namely, a being with all the characteristics of the Being which was thought of, but which in addition existed. Thus God belongs to class 1. He is thought of *and* exists in reality.

Such is the reasoning of the first ontological argument, unconvincing yet seemingly irrefutable. However, we *can* refute it, as follows: The argument does in fact show that the term "God" as traditionally defined cannot apply to anything which does not exist in reality. Thus, if anyone uses the term "God" to refer to a being which exists only in the mind, or which at one time existed but no longer exists in reality, he either contradicts himself or has altered the traditional definition of the term "God." But if we deny that the term "God" refers to *anything,* existent *or* nonexistent, we do not contradict ourselves. Thus the ontological argument fails, for all it shows is that if the term "God" has *any* reference, that reference must be to a really existing being. But we can deny that the term "God" has any reference.

On the positive side of the ledger is the fact that the ontological argument shows that theologians who have said that "God is dead" are either talking nonsense or are using the term "God" in a way completely different from the traditional sense. To say that God once existed but exists no longer is either to contradict oneself, or to covertly change the traditional understanding of the term. Thus, those who say such things are open to an objection: "If you are using the term in the usual sense what you say is false; if you are using it in some special sense of your own, what you say is trivial."

But on the negative side, the ontological argument fails to "adequately establish the existence of a being which is properly called 'God.' " Furthermore, we can see that *any* argument of this general form is open to the same fatal objection: No matter how much we pack into the definition of our terms, it is always possible to simply raise the possibility that these terms fail to have a referent. And no term can guarantee that it has a referent—how could it?

Descartes's version of the ontological argument may at first appear to escape this objection. Descartes argues that we have an idea of God and that an idea must be based on something which has at least as much reality as the idea. Of course we have ideas of such things as pink elephants or hobbits, but we have experienced real elephants and real pink objects, and we can account for our idea of pink elephants by saying that we take the color from the real pink objects, the other characteristics from the real elephants, and mentally combine them. Fictional beings, like J. R. R. Tolkein's hobbits, can be accounted for by a somewhat more complicated version of the same process. But, Descartes argues, how could we have the idea of an all-powerful, all-knowing, perfectly good being, since we have had no experience of such a being? Descartes concludes that we could have gotten our idea of God only if it was put in our minds by God Himself, and thus the very fact that we have an idea of God shows that God must exist!

Like Anselm's ontological argument, this is ingenious, but not really convincing. If we really had a full, detailed idea of God of a sort which could not be explained on the basis of any of our other experiences, Descartes's argument might have some force. But it seems that most characteristics attributed to God, such as being all-powerful and all-knowing, can be understood on the basis of our everyday experience: taking ordinary ideas of power and knowledge and mentally removing the limitations from those ideas. Many of our names for God, such as Father, Maker, Ruler, are understood by analogies or comparisons with objects of our ordinary experience. It would be granted by many religious believers that we could get the *idea* of God from experiences of the things God has made, just as we can get some idea of an author from reading his books, without ever having met him.

But, just as in the case of Anselm's argument, there is something to be gained for the religious believer from our examination of this argument. We do seem to be able to understand and deal with the idea of a being who has the characteristics which have been traditionally attributed to God. If all of our knowledge comes from experience, then it must be granted that experience has given many people the idea of such a being, and that experience may suggest reasons for or against the existence of such a being. If, on the other hand, the idea of God is not suggested by experience, we must account for it in some other way, and Descartes's argument gives a possibility which must be considered.

An analogy might help: Suppose we encountered a remote and isolated tribe who had legends about animals with all the characteristics of lions, even though we were sure that lions had never lived in their area. If the tribe's legends described lions as living in their area in the past we might conclude that these legends were mistaken, though if we did so we would have to consider alternative explanations of how they got the idea of a lion. But it would be silly to argue that the legends could not be evidence for lions in the area because the people had no real idea of what a lion was, and that they had no real idea of what a lion was because they had never seen a lion. The very fact that they can describe something recognizable to us as a lion, and that we can debate whether the legends are invention or based on real lions in the area in the past, or borrowed from peoples who *had* seen lions, etc., means that they have an idea of what a lion is.

Similarly, the very widespread idea of a God in human societies may be an invention, or an extension of ideas gained from ordinary experience or somehow, directly or indirectly, derived from a real God. But the very fact that we can debate these issues shows that we have some idea of what we mean by "God." Those philosophers who try to argue that we cannot talk about God because our idea of God is not "based on experience," often seem to have a very narrow idea of how an idea can be based on experience, which lays them open to Descartes's argument that if our idea of God did not come from experience, it must have come from God Himself! They may attempt to deny that we have a real idea of God, but the very fact we can argue about God's existence is evidence that we attach some meaning to the idea.

The whole question of what we mean when we talk about God is part of the complex issue of religious language, which we will look at in a later chapter. But for the moment we will conclude our discussion of the ontological argument by saying that although it does not seem that we can prove the existence of God from the idea or definition of God, nevertheless there are questions about the nature and origin of our idea of God which need answering.

We might lead into our discussion of the religious experience argument by noting that some philosophers have argued that our idea of God *is* based directly on experience, that in prayer and certain other states we have a direct experience of God. Some people would claim that we can make direct contact with God by prayer or other religious practices, and that having made such contact we no longer need to *argue* that God exists—we know by experience that He does! We will leave these special states called "mystical experiences" for discussion in a later chapter; these are supposedly extraordinary and unusual experiences that only some religious believers have. What we will consider here is the argument based on experiences which, it is claimed, all, or almost all, religious believers have or can have.

Various descriptions are given of these experiences. Sometimes religious believers experience great joy or peace when praying or engaging in other religious practices. Sometimes during prayer the believer will have a very vivid sense of God's being present. Or there will be a sense of "rightness" or divine approval when performing acts commanded by the believer's religion.

A very common criticism of the attempt to base the existence of God on such experiences as we have briefly described is the following: Since it would be possible to have such experiences even if God did not exist, we cannot conclude from the existence of these experiences that God does exist. We would be justified in accepting the existence of God on the basis of such experiences only if God were the *only* explanation for them.

It can be granted that if there were experiences such that God's action was the *only* possible explanation for them, we would have a very strong argument for the existence of God. But it does not follow that because God is not the only explanation of certain experiences, they provide no evidence at all for the existence of God. God's action might still be the *best* explanation of such experiences. That Lee Harvey Oswald shot President Kennedy is not the *only* explanation of what happened in Dallas in 1963. But if it is the *best* explanation, we may well be justified in regarding Oswald as guilty.

The question then becomes one about competing explanations of religious experience: What are the possible explanations, and which one is to be preferred? The explanation most frequently offered as an alternative to the religious believer's interpretation of these experiences is psychological. According to this kind of explanation the feelings of joy, peace, etc., experienced by some religious believers during prayer, for example, are the result of factors in the development of the individual, and there is no need to bring in any supernatural reality to explain them. The most powerful argument for this kind of psychological claim is that very similar, if not identical, experiences are claimed by persons with no religious beliefs, and occur in completely nonreligious contexts. Say, for example, that a religious believer experiences a feeling of intense joy and peace during prayer and meditation, but that an atheistic mathematician has an experience which seems to be very similar, or even identical, while relaxing one evening with a drink, a cigar, and an interesting new treatise on his mathematical specialty. If the experiences are the same, or even very similar, and the mathematician's experience can be explained in nonreligious terms, then it seems likely that the religious believer's experience can also be explained in nonreligious terms.

Of course, many religious believers would indignantly reject the notion that the joy and peace experienced by the mathematician was the same as, or even very much like, the joy and peace experienced by the believer in prayer. And since we have a very limited vocabulary for describing such states, and there seems to be no way of objectively measuring such things as joy and peace, the dispute is a very difficult one to settle.

Perhaps, then, what we need is some standard other than quality and intensity of experience, since these are so difficult to assess. It might be claimed by the religious believer that genuine religious experiences can be known as such by their *effects*: Having such experience makes one more loving, more humble, more resistant to temptation, etc. The critic may reply that character-improving experiences also occur to non-believers and in nonreligious contexts. If the believer concedes that these secular experiences are not evidence for the existence of God, he must admit the possibility that similar religious experiences are not evidence for the existence of God.

Consider an example: A young mountain climber gets up early one morning and sees sunrise over a range of mountains. He experiences intense joy and peace, and forms a resolve to spend his whole life helping others to enjoy the mountains. Something in the beauty of the mountains makes him feel insignificant and unworthy, and he resolves to behave better toward other people in his everyday life as well as in mountain-climbing situations. There is no thought of God in his mind; he is and remains an agnostic. He has no sense of being in contact with any personal being as part of his experience; it is purely an appreciation of mountains as natural objects of great beauty. Surely this experience of the mountaineer is not evidence that God exists, and surely it is very much like many experiences which are described by religious believers. But if the mountaineer's experience is explainable naturalistically, without bringing in God, why is the same not true of the believer's experience?

If someone is already a believer he may want to claim that even experiences like the mountaineer's are "sent by God" in some way. But that is not the question; rather, the question is one of evidence. If one of two very similar experiences is not evidence for God's existence, how can the other be? This is about as much as can be said from a general, purely philosophical, point of view. The problem now becomes one of looking at religious experiences and the allegedly similar nonreligious experiences in detail, a task too complicated for an introductory book such as this. We will, however, take another look at religious experience as compared with drug experiences in Chapter 8 of this book, and we will take that opportunity to explore these issues somewhat more fully.

When we come to the moral argument for the existence of God we find problems somewhat similar to those we have just discussed in connection with religious experience. We have moral experiences of guilt, of feeling responsibility, of admiration for goodness, of indignation at evil. Is the existence of God the only explanation, or at least the best explanation, of these moral experiences? Religious believers have often claimed that purely naturalistic explanations of our moral experiences account for them only in the sense of explaining them away. If our feelings of guilt or responsibility, for example, are given a psychological or sociological explanation, there would seem no good reason to pay attention to such feelings. If my feelings of guilt for hurting or killing someone is only a conditioned response which I have because of social training or childhood upbringing, why should I not recondition myself to overcome such feelings? After all, as we grow up we throw off much of our childhood conditioning about such things as food and clothing; probably most of us have learned to like foods our parents disliked, and clothing and hair styles often change drastically from generation to generation. If morality is simply social custom or childhood conditioning, why not change it to suit ourselves?

Similar conclusions seem to follow from other naturalistic accounts of morality. If our feeling that murder is wrong can be explained by a psychological mechanism similar to those which produce neuroses and psychoses, why not "cure" ourselves of morality as we try to cure ourselves of psychoses and neuroses? Similarly, even if morality can be explained as due to deep instinctual drives in human beings, why not try to modify or eliminate these, just as people training to be a fire-fighter must try to control or eliminate their "natural" fear of fire and heights?

Of course, what we have said so far is only an objection if we do not agree that morality can be changed to suit ourselves. The whole question of the objectivity of our moral experience, whether there is a real right and wrong about such things as murder, is a complex matter, and we cannot do justice to it here. However, a good many people who have thought seriously about the matter have come to the conclusion that the existence of God and the objectivity of morality are tied together: If God doesn't exist, there is no objective morality; but equally, if there is a genuinely objective morality, God must exist. Thus, if we can be convinced that morality is objective then we have an argument for the existence of God.

Not everyone, however, would agree that there is this kind of tie between God and objective morality. Some philosophers have argued that moral truths are somehow self-evident to our minds; others have thought that morality can somehow be based on a fundamental human nature common to all human persons. The religious believer argues in reply that if there is no God, then our human nature, and also the minds which are alleged to see the self-evidence of moral truths, are simply the result of mindless forces working accidentally or in accordance with some inherent nonintelligent pattern. If that is the origin of our nature and our minds, how can we reasonably take our nature as a guide, or trust what our minds tell us is self-evident? We might just as well make moral decisions by flipping a coin; for if there is no God, what nature we have or how our minds work is as accidental or unintended as the outcome of a coin toss.

Perhaps the most plausible naturalistic theory of morality is the one which bases morality on the need of human beings for communication, cooperation, and affection. This theory points out that such basic notions of morality as not harming others, keeping commitments, etc., are really the basic rules for getting along with other human beings, and if we do not follow them we will be cut off from the affection, cooperation, and even the communication with others which we need to make us happy. (Some supporters of this theory give an evolutionary account of how these needs developed, but this is not essential for our present purposes.)

There are difficulties with this theory as an explanation of morality. For example, it does not seem to explain cases of self-sacrificing love where, for instance, a person gives up his life for another; for if I give up my life how can I satisfy *any* needs, including the needs for affection, etc., which are supposed to be the basis of my moral choices? A theory which can be regarded as an ingenious attempt to turn such difficulties into a special kind of moral argument for the existence of God was given by the German philosopher, Immanuel Kant, in the eighteenth century.

Kant began by arguing that we cannot desire something if we know that it is impossible. He then argued that at the very foundation of morality is the desire for what he called a "kingdom of ends": a state of affairs where each person is regarded and treated as an "end in himself"—that is, as important for his own sake, not just as a means to someone else's purposes or ends. Kant then tried to show that a universe which was created, or at least ruled, by a morally good God, was the only kind of universe in which a "kingdom of ends" was really possible. So, Kant argued, the existence of a good, all-powerful God is necessary for the possibility of the kingdom of ends, the possibility of the kingdom of ends is necessary for morality, and therefore the existence of God is necessary for morality.

Kant's own version of the argument is very much tied up with the assumptions of his own philosophical system, but the basic insight of this argument seems to many people to have some force. Only if God exists, they feel, can we really hope for a morally satisfactory outcome to our human strivings and sufferings. To reject God is to say that our moral feelings are a "useless passion," a longing for what can never be. If this is true, then it at least shows one of the costs of rejecting religious belief: We cannot both reject God and have an attitude of moral optimism, the attitude that things will work out justly or fairly in the end. To see that these things go together at least forces us to count the cost of the rejection of religious belief, to see that we should not lightly or without strong reasons deny that God exists.

Two sources of confusion about the relation of religion to morality should perhaps be mentioned here. The simpler source of confusion is the idea that the only kind of religious morality is that which thinks that moral laws are simply arbitrary commands of God—that God arbitrarily orders us to love and help others, but might just as well have ordered us to hate and hurt others and that hatred and hurting would then be good.

Although some religious believers have seemed at times to hold such a view, it is not the view held by most religious believers who have given serious thought to the question. Even those who seem to hold this view may be confusing it with the much more defensible view that *some* actions are morally right simply because God has commanded them. Given that traffic must flow in some reasonable pattern, the state can decree that everyone will drive on the right side of the road. It might just as well have been the left side, as it is in England, but some decision had to be made and since it has been made it would be wrong to drive on the left in America. Similarly, God can give specific commands which are binding: Given the relation of human beings to God, worship is appropriate, but how often and on what occasions public worship should be offered is a matter of commands which could be changed. Christians, for example, believe that the command to worship God publicly every Saturday, found in the Old Testament, has been changed into a command to worship God publicly (in certain ways not found in the Old Testament) on Sundays.

But although the state can issue commands and prohibitions by its legitimate authority, the law is not founded on an arbitrary command, but on the welfare of the peoples in the state. Similarly, most religious thinkers have believed that although God can give commands and prohibitions which are binding on us just because they are God's commands and prohibitions, the moral law in general is not based on arbitrary commands and prohibitions, but on the nature of God and the nature of man.

This leads to a second and deeper sort of misunderstanding about the relation of God and morality. The following argument is often heard: "If morality is not just God's arbitrary command, there must be some standard by which we judge God's commands to be right. But if there is such a standard we don't need God in order to have objective morality, we can simply apply that standard directly to actions."

The argument sounds plausible; why have I called it a misunderstanding? Because it mistakes the relation of the standard of morality to God. In the view we have been discussing, God's nature, revealed in His actions, is itself the standard of morality, and it could not be such a standard unless God existed. Consider the following parallel: If a young girl who had never seen skating were to see Dorothy Hamill's Olympic Gold Medal performance, she might be inspired to become a skater, and could use Dorothy Hamill as a standard of excellence in skating. If the girl merely imagined an ideal skater, her imagined figure could not serve as a standard in the same way.

For the believer in a historically-based religion, of course, that history itself gives a certain standard with which to compare actions; the Jew will use God's goodness to Israel, His Patience and mercy toward a people who often betrayed Him, as a standard against which to measure one's own actions toward others. The Christian will see Christ as a pattern of moral perfection and try to imitate Him. If the allegedly historical facts about Israel or about Christ were merely myths, the believer could not *learn* about morality from them; he would only be putting his already held ideas into the myths.

One way to express this is to say that religion gives the believer certain *paradigm cases* of morality; for instance, a Christian might learn what loving concern *is* by hearing the story of the Good Samaritan. The question now becomes this: Are such paradigm cases only accidentally paradigmatic—that is, could cases taken from a nonreligious context have served the *same* purpose? But this brings us back to the question of what morality is. If it is something objective, we can recognize the same quality in different instances, as we can recognize redness or roundness in different instances. But what is it that we are recognizing when we recognize moral goodness? If moral goodness is an expression of God's nature in the world, then any recognition of goodness is a recognition which leads us back to God—and this is just what the religious believer claims.

Could there be a *nonpersonal* objective goodness? Some Eastern religions such as Taoism seem to suggest such a view; they talk of "The

Way," "The Tao" seemingly as nonpersonal. The Western religious believer argues that although the source of morality may be *more* than personal it cannot be *less* than personal, and this is a dispute we will look at in our chapter on Eastern religion. But for the moment we will conclude this discussion by noting that for the religious believer a standard of morality independent of God makes no sense, for his standard is the nature of God.

Most of the discussion among philosophers about the existence of God has centered on arguments which try to show that an intelligent Creator, or at least Designer, is the best explanation for the existence and the apparent orderliness and understandability of the universe—the kind of arguments mentioned by Mr. Larrigan in our story. Some religious believers now reject this sort of argument as a misunderstanding of the part God plays in our thinking. Giving the traditional kind of argument for the existence of God, they think, shows a misunderstanding of the difference between science and religion, and presupposes an outmoded view of the universe. Other religious believers disagree and still defend the traditional arguments.

Thus the whole question of how far we can trust arguments for the existence of God from the nature of the universe is entangled with issues of the relation of science to religion as well as with issues of what is meant by some of the language we use to discuss God. These complicated questions deserve a chapter to themselves, and we will give them one.

DISCUSSION QUESTIONS

1. Do you think the existence of God is a matter on which we can give evidence or arguments? Why or why not?
2. Can *you* give any arguments for or against the existence of God? State the argument or arguments as clearly as possible.
3. Do you find either version of the ontological argument convincing? If so, how would you defend it against criticisms? If not, what do you think is wrong with it?
4. How would you account for the kind of religious experiences discussed in this chapter? Defend your answer.
5. How is morality related to religion? (Are they independent; does one depend on the other?) Defend your answer.
6. What in your view is the best explanation of moral experience?
7. Which argument in this chapter seems to you to be strongest? Why?

8.   Which argument in this chapter seems to you to be weakest? Why?

9.   Do you have any further criticisms of any of the arguments in this chapter? State them as clearly as you can.

10.   Do you have any other arguments, or versions of arguments, for the existence of God which are not in this chapter? State them as clearly as you can.

SUGGESTED READINGS

BRODY, BARUCH, ed., *Readings in the Philosophy of Religion*. Englewood Cliffs, N.J.: Prentice-Hall, Inc., 1974:

Ontological Argument:

PLANTINGA, ALVIN, "Kant's Objection to the Ontological Argument," pp. 28–31.

ST. ANSELM, "The Presentation of the Argument," pp. 12–14.

Religious Experience:

MARTIN, C. B., "A Religious Way of Knowing," pp. 516–21.

Moral Argument:

BRODY, BARUCH A., "Morality and Religious Reconsideration."

NOWELL-SMITH, PATRICK, "Morality, Religious and Secular."

HICK, JOHN H., *Philosophy of Religion*, 2d ed. Englewood Cliffs, N.J.: Prentice-Hall, Inc., 1973:

Ontological Argument, Chapter 2, pp. 16–19.

Moral Argument, p. 28.

Religious Experience, p. 29.

YANDELL, KEITH, ed., *God, Man and Religion*. New York: McGraw-Hill Book Company, 1973:

Ontological Argument:

GAUNILON, "A Critique of Anselm," pp. 399–402.

ST. ANSELM, " 'God Exists' is a Necessary Truth," pp. 397–98.

ST. ANSELM, "A Reply to Gaunilon," pp. 403–13.

Moral Argument:

KANT, IMMANUEL, "The Moral Argument," p. 485.

Religious Experience:

BROAD, C. D., "The Argument from Religious Experience," pp. 113–21.

4

Knowledge of God:

Is God Really Dead?

As the background music died down, Reverend Ray McMackin looked into the camera and smiled. "Welcome to Lifeline, a program of religious discussion. Tonight our guests are Professor Gene Urban, from the Graduate School of Theology at our State University, and Father Augustine De Casa of the Department of Philosophy at Xavier University. Our topic tonight is a reassessment of the theological movement called 'Christian Atheism' or the 'Death of God' movement. While these ideas no longer command as much interest in the news media as they once did, they are still very much with us in some ways. Tonight we'd like to get a better understanding of this movement and its present influence on theology. Perhaps Dr. Urban, who is in sympathy with this movement, would start us off by briefly explaining what is meant by the 'Death of God.'"

In repose Urban's longish hair and casual clothes had made him look a bit like a student who had wandered on to the panel by mistake, but as he began to speak McMackin was impressed by his quiet confidence. "I can only give my interpretation, because it seems to me that very different things are meant by different people. I can try to explain what I mean by it, and I'll try to do so as clearly and briefly as possible. I accept a reality which is 'wholly other'—completely different from anything we ordinarily experience—and which is the 'ground of being'—the foundation of our existence. But I don't want to use the word 'God' for that reality because that word historically has meant something which is *not* 'wholly other,' something which is *a* being and not the ground of being. What I mean by the 'death of God' is that in past history people could conceive of 'the wholly other,' the 'ground of being' in terms of a 'God,' but modern man can no longer conceive of that reality in terms of a 'God.' A mythological 'God' of the traditional kind can no longer play a serious part in our intellectual life. Some theologians have chosen to express this in mythical language by saying that 'there was once a God, but now God is dead.' What *I* would mean by this is that pre-modern man could think in terms of a 'God,' modern man cannot. Of course, children are in a sense pre-modern; a child can still think in those terms, but as we grow up we move away from mythology. First we lose Santa Claus, then we lose the traditional 'God.' We could express this mythically by saying that God is still alive for children, but if we are to grow up, this God must die for us.

"I'd also want to distinguish between belief and faith. The traditional God could be 'believed in' as we believe in a scientific theory or an historical hypothesis, but we can 'believe in' the ground of being because it is 'wholly other.' We can have faith in it, but that is quite different."

De Casa's heavily lidded eyes were fixed on Urban as he smoothly cut in, "May I ask a question about what you've said? Is 'modern man' supposed to be a descriptive or an evaluative term?"

"I beg your pardon?" replied Urban, thrown somewhat off stride. "But surely," said De Casa with a lift of his eyebrows, "modern man can't just mean 'man born in the twentieth century,' or even 'man familiar with modern thought,' because I meet any definition of *that* kind and I believe in God in just the sense of 'believe in' and 'God' which you want to rule out. Now you *could* mean by 'modern man' just a man who can't believe in God in that sense. Then I wouldn't be a modern man, and it would just be true by definition that 'modern man' can't believe in God. But defining your terms in that way wouldn't prove anything important. Do you want to say that there's something desirable or favorable about being a modern man? In other words, is 'modern man' for you a term with a built-in favorable evaluation?"

"It's not a question of favorable or unfavorable evaluation," replied Urban, "we can't help being modern men."

De Casa smiled. "I can't help being born in the twentieth century, but I can certainly help being unable to believe in God; I do believe in God. Therefore, I can believe in God."

Urban seemed somewhat nonplussed. "But you can't really; you may insist on using the old terms but you can't use them with the old meaning."

De Casa shrugged. "It's no use saying I can't when I do; I mean just the same by God as St. Paul meant or as St. Thomas Aquinas meant, and I believe in God in just the same sense they did."

"Well," said Urban a little impatiently, "if you believe in God in the way Aquinas did, it's only by deliberately putting yourself back in Aquinas's mental universe, by not coming of age as a modern man."

De Casa was unruffled. "But now we're back at the question of the evaluative force of terms like 'modern man' and 'coming of age.' You deny any evaluative force to such terms but you imply that I *ought* to be modern, *ought* to 'come of age,' and suggest that there's something wrong if I don't. But you've given me no reasons for these evaluations. I can just as well play that game and attach favorable evaluations to terms like 'traditional' or 'orthodox' and then complain because you aren't sufficiently 'traditional' or 'orthodox.' What you owe me is a *reason* for being 'modern.'"

McMackin drew a breath but wasn't quite sure how to interrupt. Twenty-five minutes more to go and already something almost like a quarrel between his panelists. Why had he ever wanted to be the host of a discussion show!

This story raises two related questions: first, the question of whether people today can still believe in God in the traditional way, and if so on what grounds; second, the question of how we can talk about God. Must we think of God as so different from anything we have experienced that none of our language can apply to Him? The two questions are related because at least some religious believers now feel that the traditional ways of proving the existence of God were not only unsuccessful but also rested on a mistake about the whole nature of religious belief.

We have already seen some kinds of attempts to prove the existence of God: the ontological argument, the argument based on religious experience, and the moral argument. Experiences which could be called "religious experiences" or "moral experiences" were seen as in need of explanation, and it was argued that the existence of God was the best explanation of those experiences.

Other traditional arguments proceeded in much the same way. Some aspect of the universe was pointed out and God's existence was offered as an explanation for it. For example, the question was raised, "Why does the physical universe exist?" and the question was answered by arguing that it must have been brought into existence by God. Or to the question, "Why does the universe behave in an apparently orderly, predictable, and understandable fashion?" God as Designer of the universe was offered in answer.

Recently a number of Christian theologians have challenged the whole basis of these traditional proofs. They have argued that using God as an explanation of elements of our experience makes the existence of God merely a sort of scientific theory. Those theologians often criticize the traditional proofs, arguing that they fail to give good grounds for accepting the existence of a God even on this level. But their real objection is that God cannot be used as an explanation of the universe without putting Him on the same level as the universe. God, they say, must be completely above and separate from the universe. "Wholly other" is a term often used.

To the many people still convinced by the traditional proofs, this seems to be an attempt to have your cake and eat it too: to evade criticisms of the traditional proofs by calling them irrelevant while still retaining an idea of God shaped by these proofs. Or, if the idea of God as *wholly* other is really taken seriously, these theologians seem to be trying to talk about something which on their own account they cannot possibly have anything to say about. If God is really *wholly* other, no language would apply to Him and we could not even think coherently about Him. So in what sense could we believe in or have faith in something we had no idea of?

The view that God is wholly other is not the only support given for the view that "God is dead." The phrase itself was first used by the German philosophers Schopenhauer and Nietzsche, who based their view that we must reject the traditional idea of God partly on a critique of the traditional arguments for God and partly on philosophical views of their own which we discuss briefly in the Capsule History of the Philosophy of Religion at the end of this book. More recently the slogan "God is dead" has been used by a school of Christian theologians who call themselves "Christian atheists." Such Christian atheists as Vahanian, Altizer, and Hamilton differ among themselves as to just what is meant by saying that "God is dead." They sometimes seem, like Gene Urban in our story, to be rejecting only certain language about God or certain conceptions of God, but sometimes their language suggests an actual death of God as an event in history.

These claims are hard to assess since the Christian atheists seem to assume rather than argue that the traditional idea of God and arguments for God must be rejected. The more traditional religious believer rejects this assumption and therefore must reject or at least reinterpret much of what the Christian atheists say about how religion must be reformulated in the light of the alleged death of God. The objections of the traditional believer are based partly on considerations like those mentioned in connection with the ontological argument: Any being who could intelligibly be said to die could not be the God of traditional belief. But the traditional believer also may challenge the rejection of the traditional arguments for God. Such arguments still seem to many believers to give good grounds for accepting God's existence and to give us at least a limited insight into God's nature.

To settle the dispute between the defenders and the critics of the traditional arguments, then, we must look first at the arguments themselves and then at the question of how "other" we must conceive of God as being, and how language and concepts can apply to God at all. Let us begin with the arguments. A defender of the traditional arguments for God's existence might argue as follows: * We must start by considering a question most people have thought of at one time or another: How did the universe as we know it begin (if it did begin)? There are three possible answers to this question:

1. The universe simply popped into existence, after a period in which nothing at all existed.
2. The universe as we know it—that is, a universe composed mainly of material objects spread out throughout space—has always existed, although it may have changed in many ways.
3. The universe of material objects in space began to exist at some time, and was brought into existence by something nonmaterial and nonspatial.

The real choice, of course, is between the second and third alternatives, for hardly anyone takes the first alternative seriously. Because it will be useful later, we will briefly see why the first alternative is so implausible. One thing we could argue about the possibility that the universe simply came into existence from nothing is that "nothing comes from nothing." We could point out that if things had simply popped into

* This argument, which is a combination of the traditional "cosmological" and "teleological" arguments, is a shortened version of an argument given in more detail in Chapter 7 of my book *Reason to Believe* (Grand Rapids, Michigan: William B. Eerdman's Publishing Company, 1974). A similar argument is discussed in Chapter 1 of my book *Philosophically Speaking* (Englewood Cliffs, N.J.: Prentice-Hall, Inc., 1975).

existence at the beginning of the universe, there would be no reason why they should not do so now. We could go on to argue that no one would take seriously the idea that anything—a dog, a table, even a grain of sand—had simply popped into existence from nothing. The impossibility of this sort of thing is a basic assumption of any rational thinking about the universe. For if any explanation of the existence of any particular thing may be just "it popped into existence for no reason," and if the ultimate explanation of everything is just that, then all explanation is undermined, as we will argue in more detail later. The second alternative is not, on the face of it, open to the same sort of objection. It seems to be possible for A to be caused by B, for B to be caused by C, and so on, backards ad infinitum. There is, however, a very serious objection to this sort of "infinite regress," as it is called.

Consider any series where A depends on B, B depends on C, and so on. We can describe such series in a general way by saying that they are cases where A has a certain property (that is, a certain thing, a certain quality, etc.) only if B has it, B has it only if C has it, and so on. For example, if A tries to borrow a typewriter from B, and B replies, "I don't have one but I'll borrow one from my friend C," and C says, "I don't have one but I'll borrow one from my friend D," and so on, this is a case of the kind we are concerned with. Or if A, a soldier, asks B, his superior officer, for permission to take a furlough and B says, "I can't give you permission without asking my superior officer, C," and C says, "I can't give you permission to give A permission unless I ask my superior officer, D," and so on, we have a case of this sort.

Now in these ordinary cases two things are clear:

1. If the series of things which don't have the property in question goes on to infinity, the first individual never gets that property. If *everyone* asked says, "I don't have a typewriter, but I'll ask . . ." A never gets his typewriter. If *every* superior officer asked says, "I can't give you permission but I'll ask . . ." then A never gets his furlough.
2. If the first thing *does* get the property in question then the series came to an end, and did *not* go on to infinity. If A gets his typewriter, someone along the line had a typewriter without having to borrow one. If A gets his furlough, some superior officer could give permission without having to ask someone else.

Let us now apply this general pattern to the existence of particular things. My existence, for example, depends on the existence of my parents, their existence on the existence of their parents, and so on. Eventually we come to a human being whose existence has to be accounted for by some cause other than procreation by other human beings, but whatever the details of this series, it is evidently a dependent series.

And if so, then it would seem that if the series were an infinite regress, I would not exist, and since I do exist the series must have had a begining. What sort of beginning? Plainly, a thing which exists whether or not anything else exists, for nothing else would put an end to a series of this kind. A being which exists whether or not anything else exists would, of course, always exist. A being of this kind is traditionally called a *necessary* being. Thus, if we can rule out an infinite regress in the realm of existence, we arrive at the existence of a necessary being, a being which always exists whether anything else exists or not.

Now God, as pictured by traditional religious belief, is a necessary Being; He exists whether or not anything else exists, and He always exists. So if we can prove the existence of a necessary being, we have made a step toward proving the existence of God, just as if we were trying to prove the existence of *intelligent* life on Mars, we would have made a step forward if we were to prove the existence of *any form of* life on Mars.

But have we proved the existence of a necessary being? It is clear that any series of causes is a dependent series, for part of what we mean by saying that A was caused by B is that A would not have existed unless B had. It is clear enough that in almost any other dependent series we can think of, the two principles we have discussed apply. Thus, to deny that they apply to the case of causes is to be inconsistent, unless we can show that this case is different from the others in some way. To be inconsistent, to say that a principle applies in one case but not in another case which is similar in all relevant respects, is to abandon reason. So we must either find a difference in the causal case or deny that the principles apply to any case. The second course would be unreasonable, but it would not have the same disastrous effects on our reasoning that accepting the "pop" theory would.

However, it might be claimed that the second group of cases are all cases which go forward in time. "All that your arguments prove," it might be claimed, "is that if we try to explain A by B, B by C, and so on, we would never reach the end of explanation. But this is all right, since each thing in the series would have an explanation." There are several replies to this. First, it is not clear that any of the cases really depend on the direction in time. If, before trying to borrow the typewriter, A is told that *no one* has a typewriter unless he can borrow one, he knows that he will never get a typewriter. If an army is set up in such a way that no superior officer can give permission for a furlough without asking someone else for it, we know that no furlough will be given.

It might be claimed that in an infinite regress, "each thing in the series will have an explanation," but this would be equally true if our explanations were circular, if we explained A by B, B by C, and C by A.

However, this is obviously unsatisfactory, so the mere fact that "each thing in the series has an explanation" does not mean that we have a satisfactory explanation for the first term in the series. But it is important to remember that the argument was in terms of existence, not in terms of explanation of existence: Unless the argument is mistaken, then if there is an infinite regress of causes I do not exist, and since the same argument can be applied to anything, nothing exists. Which is absurd.

However, it is *possible* to reject the conclusion that a necessary being must exist without, seemingly, rejecting reason. We can say that there is *something* different about this case even though we can't put our finger on it. We can say that the impossibility of infinite regress in the other case is due to some special features of those cases. So if someone is not convinced by the argument, there seems to be an impasse.

Let us try to avoid this impasse by going ahead a bit on the assumption that a necessary being does exist, and asking what sort of being this would be. Could the necessary being just be the material universe itself? No, for the material universe is just a collection of things, none of which is necessary, and the property of always existing whether or not anything else exists is not the sort of property which can be reached by simply adding things together which lack this property. We can get a thing which weighs a ton by adding together lots of things which do not weigh a ton, but we cannot get a thing which is transparent by adding things which are not transparent. In cases where we can get a property by adding, we get nearer to it by even small additions: Two things which weigh a pound each put together are *nearer* a ton than either separately. But two opaque things together are no more transparent than either separately, and two things which exist only because other things do are no nearer existing necessarily together than apart.

Could the necessary being be the basic "stuff" of the universe? Suppose that it were. This would solve one of our difficulties, since it would answer the question as to why anything exists at all. The answer would be that the basic stuff of the universe (matter, energy, or whatever it is) exists whether or not anything else exists. But it would not answer the question as to why any particular thing—for example, you or I or the planet we live on—exists. To explain this without bringing in God, we would have to fall back on other theories. The existence of particular things would have to be explained by chance combinations of the basic stuff, or by some "natural necessity" somehow built into that stuff.

Incidentally, we can see that the infinite regress theory is open to the same objection. Even if the general answer to the question "Why does anything exist?" is "Because something existed at some previous time," this does not give us an answer to the question "Why do the particular things that exist now exist?" To say that it is because certain particular things existed at a previous time, and that certain causal laws operated to bring about the present state of affairs, is simply to push the difficulty back to the previous states of affairs and the laws.

We are faced, in fact, with a problem about the nature of the universe as experience reveals it to us. That universe behaves in a regular and broadly predictable way, and we can understand many of the regularities, and use them to predict and control events. The universe, in other words, is *orderly* and *intelligible*. This orderliness and intelligibility must be explainable in one of three ways:

1.   As the result of design by a mind in some ways like ours;
2.   As the result of chance;
3.   As the result of "natural necessity."

We have already seen the difficulties inherent in the last two possibilities. But there are additional drawbacks. Consider the problems we face in decoding any apparently intelligible message. If we believe that the message is the result of intelligent design and is meant to be decoded, then we can have some hope of finding a pattern which makes sense. But if the apparent message is the result of mere chance throwing together of letters, then not only can we not expect any apparent regularities we have encountered to continue, but the supposed regularities we think we have discovered are illusory. So the result of accepting the chance theory in a consistent way would be the expectation that natural laws might cease to operate any second, and the realization that all of our apparent scientific knowledge was illusory.

The same difficulty threatens even the "natural necessity" theory. In this view any regularities in the universe might, for all we know, have as little in common with our minds as the growth of branches on a tree. In fact, of course, if we found that there was a message in the way some trees were shaped, we would immediately suspect intelligent interference: Someone must have trained or pruned the trees to carry the message. In talking about *parts* of the universe, we never assume that intelligible order "just grew."

Thus, again we have a contrast of two possible views of the universe. In the theistic view the material universe is caused by an intelligent necessary being, and this explains not only its existence but its order and intelligibility. With the "pop" theory the universe is meaningless and reason is useless. In the view that the basic stuff of the universe is necessary, we have an explanation of sorts of the *existence* of the universe, but not of its orderliness and intelligibility. And with the infinite regress theory, even if we can get over its other difficulties, we also have no explanation for the orderliness and intelligibility of the universe. We have to supplement the theory with either the chance theory or the natural necessity theory, and both have fatal difficulties. The religious believer who defends this traditional line of argument would say, then, that the view that the universe was created by God seems to be the only view that accounts for all the facts, that gives reason a place, that leads us to expect continued regularity and understandability in the universe.

Two objections may occur to you here. The first is the old difficulty "Who made God?" But if God is a necessary being, then the question has no point: No one made God; He always existed and always will, no matter what else exists or does not exist. We can also see that the usual objection to this reply, "Then why not say the universe always existed and always will no matter what else does or doesn't exist?" can be answered by what we have already said. If by the universe we mean just the collection of non-necessary things, lumping them together does not make them necessary. If we mean "the basic stuff of the universe" then we are left without an explanation of orderliness and intelligibility. Of course we could combine the theories saying that God and the basic stuff of the universe have *both* always existed, God accounting for orderliness and intelligibility. But why posit two necessary beings when one will do the job? (There are also objections to the idea of a number of independent necessary beings. What is their supposed relation? How would they affect each other?)

This, then, is one statement of the traditional line of argument for God's existence. The argument I have given is in fact a combination of several traditional arguments which are often stated separately; I have done this to give the strongest possible argument. And before we go on, it is only fair to point out that many people find some such argument or combination of arguments completely convincing; throughout history many clear and careful thinkers have been convinced of the existence of God by arguments such as these. However, it is equally true that many equally intelligent people have considered such arguments and not been convinced by them. We have already stated some particular criticism of the arguments; we will now go on to consider some more general reasons for skepticism about the success of any arguments from the universe to God.

Arguments of this kind try to show that unless God exists the universe is not rationally understandable. Perhaps such arguments are even successful in showing this. But, critics frequently ask, what grounds do we have for expecting the universe to be rationally understandable? Even if we grant that without the existence of God the universe has no ultimate explanation, why should we assume that the universe *has* an ultimate explanation?

Those who use this line of argument often point out that scientific explanations do not claim to be ultimate explanations of the universe. A scientific explanation, while it may explain phenomena in terms of laws, and the laws in terms of higher level laws or theories, always leaves something unexplained; the highest level laws and theories in terms of which other things are explained must remain unexplained themselves. Of course we may find yet higher level laws or theories, but they will be unexplained. Why not, it is argued, accept this kind of explanation as the best we can do and accept the idea that there are ultimate explanations?

To the defender of the traditional arguments for the existence of God, the critic who takes the position just described seems to be trying to have his cake and eat it too. He takes it for granted that the universe is understandable and that scientific explanations do enable us to understand the relation of phenomena to laws and of lower level laws to higher level laws and theories. But when the question of *why* the universe is understandable and predictable by science is raised, this critic suddenly gives up the quest for explanations. But if the nature of the universe as a whole cannot be rationally explained, why should we expect the details of the universe to be connected in an understandable way?

The defender of the traditional arguments might compare the situation with that of a man who tries to get out of debt by borrowing; he borrows from Peter to pay Paul, from Tom to pay Peter, from Dick to pay Tom, and from Harry to pay Dick, but then makes no effort to repay Harry. If he is content to remain in debt to Harry, why didn't he just remain in debt to Paul in the first place? So, the defender of the traditional arguments maintains, if the end of the process of seeking explanations is something we are content to leave unexplained, something which is just like the things we have tried to explain along the way, then why begin the process of explanation at all?

The critic will challenge the defender to say what an ultimate explanation, an explanation which is not itself in need of explanation, would be like. Is not the defender relying on a paradigm taken from mathematics, and an outdated kind of mathematics at that? A view of mathematics which was prevalent until fairly recently was that mathematical truths could be proved from "axioms," but that the axioms themselves were "self-evident" and could be known to be true without proof. The critic argues that the defender's search for an ultimate explanation is a search for something like a mathematical "axiom," but to expect something like this where explanations of the universe are concerned is to confuse empirical facts and mathematics.

The defender could reply that indeed what he is looking for is something like an axiom: an explanatory entity which does not itself need explanation. But the defender could challenge the critic's assumption that it is a mistake to look for something of this sort when we are dealing with empirical facts. It may or may not be justifiable to think of mathematical proofs as ultimately resting on mere postulates or assumptions. In mathematics we may sometimes just be interested in exploring the consequences of certain assumptions, but if we are trying to prove the truth of something, a line of proof that ends in an unsupported assumption will not do. We might just as well have assumed in the first place the truth of what we were supposed to be trying to prove.

The defender, in other words, is trying to convince the critic that he must choose a view which admits ultimate explanations, or else give way to skepticism. You cannot, he argues, stop halfway, call for explanations when it suits you and then refuse to look for explanations when that suits you. The critic, on the other hand, is trying to show that we can reasonably stop looking for explanations at a certain point; and in particular, he claims that the lack of ultimate explanations does not destroy the validity of nonultimate explanations.

That defenders of a scientific world-view should reject the traditional arguments for God's existence is not unexpected, but it is more surprising to find that a number of religious believers, some of them religious believers of a quite conservative and traditional kind, reject the traditional arguments with even greater vehemence. But as we have already mentioned, some religious believers reject the attempt to show the existence of God by arguing from the existence and order of the universe on the ground that it puts God on the same level as the universe. It makes Him, in one theologian's words, "merely another being rather than the Ground of Being."

Now, on the face of it, this is a curious argument. If I try to draw some conclusions about the character and interests of my favorite novelist by reading her books, does this mean that I am treating her as "merely another book" or, less absurdly, "merely a fictional character," rather than as the creator of those books and those fictional characters? We would have no tendency to say such things in that case, so why should we assume that arguing from the universe for God as Creator or Designer of the universe puts Him on the same level as His creation?

Those who want to make God "wholly other" would argue that the author and her creations are, broadly speaking, the same *sort* of things. She and her books both occupy space and have weight; she is a real human being, and her characters are fictional human beings. But God, they argue, is not at all the same *sort* of thing as any of His creations; you cannot put God and His creatures in the same class in any way.

Insofar as their arguments for this conclusion are theological, based on interpretations of scriptural passages, the philosopher as such has nothing in particular to say about them. But if one attempts to give, as some of these theologians have attempted to give, philosophical arguments in support of this conclusion, then the philosopher can criticize and perhaps refute these arguments.

One argument which is sometimes given is that God is by definition infinite or unlimited, and thus finite, limited beings like ourselves cannot understand Him. This objection can be at least partly answered by a simple distinction between comprehension, or complete understanding, and apprehension, or incomplete understanding. It is certainly true that a lesser being cannot *comprehend, fully* understand, a greater being. But it is by no means obvious that a lesser being cannot *apprehend, partly* understand, a greater, and this includes the case of a finite being's apprehending an infinite being.

What can we say in a positive way about *how* human beings might be able to partly understand God? There are two traditional approaches to this problem. The first is the analogical approach, which says that although when we speak of, for example, God's wisdom or goodness we mean something different from human wisdom or goodness, nevertheless, there is an analogy between God's wisdom and ours, God's goodness and ours. The other approach says that, for example, "wisdom" and "goodness" are *univocal*—that is, have the same meaning—as applied to human beings and to God. The difference is that God's wisdom and goodness are infinite or unlimited, whereas ours are infinite and limited.

Both views have difficulties. The difficulty often urged against the analogy view is that normally, when we say that A and B are analogous, we have to have some experience of *both* to make this judgment. But if we have no direct experience of God's wisdom or goodness, how can we say that they are analogous to ours? One answer sometimes given to this objection involves the idea of an *analogy of proportion.* In a mathematical proportion—for example, "4 is to 16 as x is to 81"—we can solve for x because we know the other three terms. Thus, it has been argued, we can say "human goodness is to human nature as God's goodness is to God's nature," and because we know about human goodness and human nature, and have at least some idea of God's nature, we can use our knowledge of these three "terms" to understand something of God's goodness, the remaining "term."

However, those who insist that successful use of analogy depends on some familiarity with both sides of the analogy will not be satisfied by this. They will argue that we have no experience of God's nature and thus we have at best two terms of the supposed "proportion" and not three.

At this point the defenders of the analogy view begin to sound more and more like defenders of the univocal view. Defenders of both views would argue that we can know that God's nature must be *infinite*, or free of limitations. Thus, our limited goodness is to our limited nature as God's unlimited goodness is to His unlimited nature, if you wish to preserve the language of analogy; or in the univocal view we can say that God's goodness and human goodness are both goodness, but that ours is limited, God's is unlimited. The analogy view and the univocal view now seem to differ mainly in their answers to the question "Is infinite goodness the *same* as finite goodness, except for its absence of limitations, or is it only *similar* to finite goodness?" The difference does not seem very deep.

Let us look briefly, then, at the idea, sometimes called the "way of remotion" that we can describe God's characteristics by removing the limitations of human characteristics which are the same (or similar) but limited. For some characteristics, such as knowledge it looks quite plausible. Our knowledge is limited; God is usually thought of as knowing everything. Our knowledge is often hard to acquire, or indirectly known. God's knowledge is thought of as immediate and direct. But a number of difficulties remain. How do we know what characteristics to start with in applying this way of remotion? It seems plausible to say that God will have all good characteristics to an infinite degree, but how do we know which characteristics are good ones? Again, what *are* the limitations on, for example, human goodness, and what does it mean to say that we can remove these limitations yet still have the same property? Some philosophers have suggested that we cannot remove the limitations from a concept such as wisdom or goodness and still have an intelligible concept.

Defenders of the way of remotion believe that they can answer such questions satisfactorily, and the debate is still going on. Both sides agree that the question of whether we can reason out God's characteristics by removing the limitations of good human characteristics is closely tied to the question of whether arguments for God based on the nature of the universe can be successful. But if such arguments are successful, then it would seem that the way of remotion can give some content to our idea of God, despite our lack of direct experience of God.

Once the idea of the way of remotion is understood, it is hard to comprehend the hostility of some religious believers to the idea that we can have an idea of the existence and nature of God by reasoning from the universe. Sometimes this hostility is based on the argument that God is infinitely greater than His creation; but this is precisely what the traditional arguments and the way of remotion say: The universe is dependent for existence, God exists independently; created goodness is finite, God's is infinite.

Within the limits of this chapter we have not been able to follow all the twists and turns of these arguments in recent philosophy; but we now at least have some idea of where the battle lines are drawn. To return to the story which opened this chapter, it is by no means obvious that someone who is "modern" merely in the sense of being born in this century must be "modern" in the sense of rejecting traditional arguments for God, or ways of looking at God. Nor is it clear that we must attach a favorable value to being "modern" in this second sense of rejecting traditional ways of thinking about God. Whether the "traditional" view is more reasonable than the "modern" view is a matter for each of us to decide for ourself, but we cannot settle the question by attaching chronological labels to one side or the other.

DISCUSSION QUESTIONS

1. If God is the Creator of the universe, does this mean that we can learn something about God from the universe? Discuss cases where we can or cannot learn something about a creator from what has been created (e.g., book/author, composer/music, sculptor/statue, etc.).
2. If God were *completely* different from us, would we be able to say or think anything about Him? Why or why not?
3. Does it ever make sense to say that something has come into existence from nothing? If not, why not? If you think it sometimes does, give and discuss a possible case of something coming from nothing.
4. What cases of dependent regress can you think of? Do the two principles discussed in this chapter apply to your case?
5. Are there any exceptions to the principle that if we can get a property by adding things which don't have that property, then each addition gets us nearer to that property? Discuss.
6. Can you think of any defenses or additional criticisms of the view that the apparent orderliness and understandability of the universe is due to chance or to "natural necessity"?
7. What is the relationship between a confidence in scientific explanation and a belief that the universe is ultimately rational? Discuss.
8. What objections might a religious believer have to the idea of reasoning from the universe to God? Are there reasonable answers to these objections? Discuss.
9. Discuss the problem of how finite beings could understand or talk about God. What are the possible solutions? What can be said for or against these solutions?
10. Discuss the ways in which we "must" be "modern," making clear how you are using key terms.

SUGGESTED READINGS

BRODY, BARUCH, ed., *Readings in the Philosophy of Religion*. Englewood Cliffs, N.J.: Prentice-Hall, Inc., 1974:

Arguments:

AQUINAS, ST. THOMAS, "The Five Ways," p. 64.
CLARKE, SAMUEL, "An Improved Version of the Argument," pp. 66–67.
HUME, DAVID, "Criticism of Clarke's Argument," pp. 67–70.
ROWE, WILLIAM L., "Two Criticisms of the Cosmological Argument," pp. 83–97.
SWINBURNE, R. G., "The Argument from Design," pp. 137–46.

Meaning of Predicates Applied to God:

ROSS, JAMES F., "Analogy and the Resolution of some Cognitivity Problems," pp. 288–307.

HICK, JOHN H., *Philosophy of Religion*, 2d ed. Englewood Cliffs, N.J.: Prentice-Hall, Inc., 1973:

Chapter 2, "Grounds for Belief in God," pp. 20–26.
Chapter 5, "Problems of Religious Language," pp. 68–83.

YANDELL, KEITH, ed., *God, Man and Religion*. New York: McGraw-Hill Book Company, 1973:

Arguments:

EDWARDS, PAUL, "A Critique of the Argument from Contingency," pp. 427–39.
HUME, DAVID, "A Critique of the Argument from Design," pp. 455–71.
TAYLOR, RICHARD, "A Reformulation of the Argument from Contingency," pp. 418–26.
TENNANT, F. R., "A Reformulation of the Argument from Design," pp. 441–54.

Meaning of Predictates Attributed to God:

ALSTON, WILLIAM P., "Tillich's Conception of a Religious Symbol," pp. 252–61.
TILLICH, PAUL, "The Meaning and Justification of Religious Symbols," pp. 247–51.

5

Miracles:

What If They Happen?

"It's a miracle," said Mrs. Kennedy, sitting up in her bed, and even as Dr. Buchan put out a cautioning hand, he knew that yesterday she wouldn't have had the strength to sit up that far. "We call it a spontaneous remission" he replied, trying to make his voice as calm as possible. "They happen sometimes, we don't know why."

But Sarah Kennedy was sure she knew why and wasn't shy about saying so. "It's the power of prayer, Doctor," she said earnestly, "the prayers of my family and Father O'Sullivan and the good Sisters. . . ."

Despite himself, Buchan was drawn into arguing with her. "I presume that other people in the hospital are being prayed for just as hard, but they haven't had recoveries like yours," he snapped.

There were tears in Mrs. Kennedy's eyes now. "Ah, Doctor, it's a mystery of God," she said. "The Lord knows that I prayed as hard for my husband Michael, and for the daughter that died young, as anyone ever prayed. But prayer is just asking and sometimes God says no. It's no virtue of mine that He's spared me this time—maybe He has a job for me to do yet."

Buchan smiled a little coldly. "Very convenient," he said.

"If you get well it's the power of prayer; if you don't it's the will of God. So whatever happens, you win."

He wondered if he'd gone too far, but he was reassured when he saw a trace of Mrs. Kennedy's old spirit in her grin. "Well, Doctor, tell me now," she said, "can *you* explain with all your great medical knowledge why a week ago I was at death's door and today I'm here taking the Mickey out of you?"

"No, I can't," he admitted, "but that isn't to say that we might not understand some day why things like this happen. The mind and body are related in ways we're only just beginning to understand."

But Mrs. Kennedy was not going to let him off so easily. "So it's faith healing, is it Doctor? But it's a funny kind of faith healing that can work on a person when she knows about as much of what's going on around her as a mackerel on ice."

Buchan got up from the edge of the bed where he had been, very unprofessionally, sitting. "No, Sarah, your case isn't faith healing and I'll admit that I don't know what it is. But these spontaneous remissions happen to people who don't pray as often as they occur to people that do, so you're not going to convert me to religion by getting up and dancing a jig. Don't overdo, and remember these things can get worse again as suddenly as they got better."

Mrs. Kennedy lay back. "Ah, you're a terrible old heathen, Doctor, but you've been a good friend to me and mine. Go off to your pills and your laboratory tests, but you won't find any explanation in them for what's happened to me." And as Dr. Buchan slipped out the door wearing an indulgent smile, she muttered to herself, "And I'll pray for your conversion too, you old devil. Though that would be a bigger miracle than this one."

Some religious believers think that miracles continue to occur; others believe that they have occurred only at specific places and times, where extraordinary needs brought forth extraordinary help from God. But even if events which cannot be explained by science do occur in some religious contexts, what do such events prove?

One traditional way of providing a rational basis for religious belief begins with arguments for the existence of God and goes on to argue that a certain body of religious beliefs can be known to be a revelation from God because miracles have been worked in support of those religious beliefs. For example, a Christian of one traditional sort, when challenged as to the basis of one of his beliefs—say the Second Coming of Christ—would cite certain words said by Christ. When asked why we should believe these words of Christ, he would cite the miracles done by Christ, and especially His Resurrection, as evidence that Christ's words were backed up or authenticated by God. And when asked why he believed that those miracles had indeed occurred, the traditional Christian would argue that if God exists miracles cannot be ruled out, and that miracle is the best or only explanation for certain events recorded by history. If challenged as to the existence of God, he would try to give arguments based on reason and experience for God's existence.

Thus, this kind of traditional Christian, whom we might call a rationalistic believer, nowhere appeals to blind faith or personal experiences not shared by unbelievers, but bases his assent to particular doctrines on authority, his acceptance of authority on the evidence of miracles, and his acceptance of miracles on philosophical arguments for God and historical arguments for the actual occurance of miracles.

Nowadays not only most nonbelievers but many people who would call themselves religious believers would challenge this way of providing a basis for religious belief. They would argue that accounts of miracles are not historically reliable and that a faith based on such accounts is open to historical and scientific objections. The traditional believer understands such objections from nonbelievers in God, but finds them puzzling from people calling themselves believers in God. For if God is the Creator and Ruler of the universe, then surely miracles are possible. Of course, if miracles were impossible, then any historical account which tells of the occurrence of miracles, as the Old and New Testaments plainly do, must be rejected as unhistorical. If miracles are tremendously improbable, then we must reject any account of them unless we get evidence of a kind which, in the nature of the case, history almost never gives us. But if God exists, miracles are not impossible, and unless we have some argument to show that they are improbable, then we cannot assume that they are. This undercuts most of the "historical" objections to miracles, for if we have no metaphysical objections, then we will have to examine the historical evidence on its merits. And if we do this we may find, as many reasonable and hardheaded men have found, that miracle is the best explanation for certain recorded events.

There may, of course, be historical objections to certain accounts of miracles—for example, one account may seem to be a mere imitation of another, or other historical evidence may render that particular supposed miracle improbable, and so on. But the general objection to miracles is not based on anything peculiar to history as such, but on philosophical grounds.

Another objection to miracles is the supposed objection from experience. Most versions of this objection trace back more or less indirectly to a famous objection by David Hume, which goes as follows:

A miracle is a violation of the laws of nature; and as a firm and unalterable experience has established these laws, the proof against a miracle, from the very nature of the fact, is as entire as any argument from experience can possibly be imagined. . . . Nothing is esteemed a miracle, if it ever happens in the common course of nature. It is no miracle that a man, seemingly in good health, should die of a sudden; because such a kind of death, though more unusual than any other, has yet been frequently observed to happen. But it is a miracle that a dead man should come to life; because that has never been observed in any age or country. There must, therefore, be a uniform experience against every miraculous event, otherwise the event would not merit the appellation. And as a uniform experience amounts to a proof, there is here a direct and full proof, from the nature of the fact, against the existence of any miracle; nor can such a proof be destroyed, or the miracle rendered credible, but by an opposite proof, which is superior.*

Now obviously we must interpret Hume's objection in such a way that it is not an objection to any unique event. After all, up to a certain date, there was "uniform experience" against a man setting foot on the moon. It must, therefore, be a certain *class* or *kind* of events we are eliminating. But what class? Miracles? But this begs the whole question. As an "argument" against the statement that miracles occur, we have the assertion that there is uniform experience against miracles—in other words, the unsupported assertion that miracles don't happen!

Put in this way the point may seem obvious, but both in Hume's original account and in modern restatements of views like Hume's the point is often concealed. Instead of saying baldly that experience shows that miracles do not occur, which is obviously question-begging in the context of this argument, the class of events which "experience proves don't happen" is described in some other way—as events which "exhibit causal irregularity" or as events which "neither obey known scientific laws nor are taken as refuting alleged scientific laws," or some similar description. But looked at carefully, all such descriptions turn out to be indirect ways of describing miracles. And to argue for the conclusion that miracles do not happen by assuming that miracles, under whatever description, don't happen is just to argue in a circle or beg the question.

This is not to deny that there could be some argument which concludes that miracles don't happen. But whatever that argument is, it must not have as one of its premises an assertion which amounts to saying that miracles don't happen, because that would be assuming what is supposed to be being proved.

Of course defenders of a Humean position would deny that they are arguing in a circle in this way. But to avoid the charge of circularity they

* David Hume, *Enquiries*, ed. L. A. Selby-Bigge (Oxford: Oxford University Press, 1955), pp. 114-15.

must show that the class of events they are claiming experience rules out is not just an indirect description of the class of miracles. So far as I can see neither Hume's own argument or any neo-Humean argument can meet the challenge.

I think that the only respectable way of interpreting what Hume says here is to take him as arguing that past experience gives us some kind of assurance that laws of nature *cannot* be suspended. (If it merely alleges that they *have never been* suspended, it is just "miracles don't happen" in a new guise.) We interpret Hume, then, as saying that experience proves that natural laws are "unsuspendable." But how *could* experience show any such thing? Any such theory must be a philosophical interpretation of experience, not the direct result of experience. So before coming to any decision on this matter, we must look at the philosophical, as well as the historical, pros and cons with regard to the question of miracles. We can distinguish two separable arguments which need to be looked at in turn: the argument *for* (the possibility of) miracles, and the argument *from* miracles (for religious belief).

The argument for miracles consists of two stages—an argument for the general possibility of miracles, and an argument for the historical actuality of certain miracles. The first stage is philosophical and can be developed fairly completely within the limits of this chapter. The second stage is historical and we can only indicate the main lines of the argument. The argument *from* miracles for religious belief also has two stages —the first stage a philosophical consideration of the evidential value of miracles, and the second stage a historical consideration of what specific beliefs the evidence of miracles supports. Again, we will try to cover the philosophical stage as completely as we can and only indicate the general lines of the historical argument.

Let us begin, then, with a definition of miracle. By a miracle we will mean an exception to the natural order of things caused by the power of God. By this we will mean very much what people mean when they define miracle as a suspension or violation of natural law, but for reasons that will become clear "exception" is preferable to the terms "suspension" or "violation," and "natural order of things" is preferable to the term "natural law." Notice that by this definition no event which occurs as part of the natural order of things, no matter how improbable or how faith-inspiring, will count as a miracle. There may be a wider and looser sense of miracle in which striking coincidences which inspire religious belief are called "miracles," but they are not miracles in the stricter and narrower sense in which we are now using that term.

Before we can speak of exceptions to the natural order of things we must believe that there *is* a natural order of things. If anyone holds that there is no natural order, that the universe is chaotic, that the apparent order and understandability of the universe is an illusion, then that person can give no meaning to the idea of miracle, for that idea depends on contrast. Before there can be exceptions there must be rules or patterns for them to be exceptions to. The progress of science gives us an enormously strong argument against the idea that the universe is chaotic and without order and pattern, and we will assume in what follows that we can speak of the universe as genuinely orderly and intelligible. But if anyone really wished to challenge this, we would have to settle that issue before going on to any argument with him either for or from miracles.

Given that the universe is orderly and understandable, however, we can ask whether this order can have exceptions and whether such exceptions could be due to the power of God. The answer to this question depends on the answer to another question. How can we account for the order and understandability of the universe? Ultimately there are only two possible answers to this question. We can account for the order of the universe by saying that the universe was made by a person, by a Being with knowledge and will, by someone who knows what he is doing and what he intends—in other words by God. And we can account for the understandability of the universe by saying that we are made in the image and likeness of the God who made the universe; our minds resemble His, however remotely. *Or* we can account for the order of the universe by saying that there is some inherent principle of order in the fundamental stuff of the universe, and account for our understanding that order by saying that our minds are the outcome of the unfolding of this inherent principle of order. In Chapter 1 we called this the Universe Ultimate View, and discussed its difficulties in detail.

Either theory, if accepted, would have consequences. If we really accepted the idea that our minds were the accidental result of the workings of mindless forces, we should be haunted by doubts as to whether our apparent understanding of the universe is illusory. Dogmatic confidence of any kind, including dogmatic confidence that certain sorts of events "can't happen" is not what we should logically expect from a Universe Ultimate view. (Of course, insofar as dogmatism is often the outcome of a feeling of uncertainty, we might explain the dogmatism psychologically.) The consequences of the God theory are rather different. Our confidence in the understanding of the universe given to us by science would be considerable, but it would not be absolute. If the natural order is the result of God's action, then sometimes God might act in such a way as to make exceptions to the natural order.

In this view an exception to the natural order would be like the exceptions we sometimes make to established rules and procedures—for example, allowing an exceptionally gifted child to skip grades or enter college without graduating from high school, or declaring a holiday on a day that would normally be a working day. We can often see that not making exceptions to rules would be unreasonable or unkind. Exceptions must, of course, be rare if rules are to be generally relied upon, but we can live perfectly well with a system of rules or procedures which have occasional exceptions. We may or may not think President Ford's pardon of ex-President Nixon wise or fair, but occasional exceptions to legal procedures, such as presidential pardon, do not make our legal system chaotic or unreliable.

Furthermore, provided that God wished to give us strong evidence that a given message has His authority behind it, there would seem to be no better way than a miracle. If I claim to have authority in a certain organization, strong evidence of my authority would be an ability to suspend the rules or make exceptions to usual procedures. You might meditate on the problem of how a God who never interfered with the working of the universe could establish a message from Himself as authoritative.

The scientist, of course, *as* a scientist, ignores the possibility of miracles, just as the lawyer, *as* a lawyer, must ignore the possibility of a presidential pardon for his client, since there is nothing he can do *as a lawyer* which will ensure a presidential pardon. A pardon is a free action by the President, which cannot be guaranteed by any legal maneuver; a miracle is a free act by God which the scientist cannot bring within *his* procedures.

A presidential pardon is like a miracle in that though the *origin* of the pardon is outside ordinary legal procedures, a pardon once granted has legal consequences. A miracle, once it has occurred, has consequences which fit into the kind of patterns scientists study: Drinking too much of the wine Christ made from water at Cana in Galilee would make a wedding guest drunk, and if a scientist had been there with his instruments he could verify, though not explain, the change and measure the alcoholic content of the wine made from water.

It is important to note that a presidential pardon is not *il*legal: It does not violate any laws. Furthermore, it does not suspend the laws in the sense that at a given time or place some laws cease to operate in all cases—as if, for example, the laws of libel were suspended in Hannibal, Missouri on the first Sunday in March, so that no libels in that place or time were punishable. Rather, an individual exception is made to the law, so that of two men convicted of the same crime at the same time, one may be pardoned and the other not. Similarly, a miracle does not *violate* the laws of nature, nor suspend them for all events at a given time or place: The water in one jar might be changed to wine and that in an adjacent jar be unchanged. Lazarus may be raised and a man in an adjacent tomb who died at the same time may remain dead.

A presidential pardon cannot be compelled by any legal means; it can only be asked for. It is a free act of the President. Similarly, a miracle cannot be brought about by scientific means; it can only be prayed for. It is a free act of God. A presidential pardon cannot be predicted from the legal facts and it does not create a precedent: A pardon may be granted in one case, and in precisely similar circumstances another request may be denied. Similarly, a miracle cannot be predicted by scientific means and it gives no scientific grounds for prediction once it has occurred: The miracle at Cana in Galilee does not increase the probability that water will change to wine in similar circumstances.

To sum up: We can imagine a different legal system in which there were no pardons and so no exceptions to the rule of law. However, our system is not such a system but rather one in which certain exceptions to the legal order, called presidential pardons, sometimes occur. Lawyers as such have no concern with presidential pardons, for they cannot predict them, bring them about, or draw any precedents for them. A presidential pardon is, you might say, supralegal and therefore of no *legal* interest. Similarly, it could be that our universe was one in which there were no exceptions to the natural order, but if traditional religious believers are right, our universe is not such a universe, but one in which certain exceptions to the natural order, called miracles, sometimes occur. Scientists, as such, have no concern with miracles, for they cannot predict them, bring them about, or draw any conclusions about the future course of nature from them. A miracle is supernatural, and therefore of no scientific interest.

We could not settle whether presidential pardons are possible by looking at the day-to-day business of the courts; rather, we must ask what kind of legal system we live under. We cannot settle whether miracles occur by looking at the ordinary course of nature; we must ask what kind of universe we live in. This is a philosophical, not a scientific, question, and one very relevant philosophical consideration is that a universe made by God leaves room for confidence in human reason, whereas a universe of natural necessity does not.

If we come to the conclusion that miracles are possible, then we must consider miracle as one possible explanation of certain events recorded in history. Again, because most readers of this book will have been influenced to some extent by Christianity, we will consider Christian claims with regard to miracles. Early Christians claimed that the tomb of Christ was empty and that Christ had risen from the dead. The Roman and Jewish authorities did not refute this claim by producing the body, as they would certainly have done had *they* removed it from the tomb. The Apostles suffered persecution, hardship, and martyrdom to proclaim the message of Christ risen from the dead, which they surely would not have done if *they* had removed and hidden Christ's body. Christians claim that no naturalistic explanation which tries to explain the disappearance of the body and the confidence of the early Christians comes anywhere near accounting for all the facts.

If miracles were impossible, we should have to try to account for the data in some other way; but there is no good argument which shows that miracles are impossible. If miracles were tremendously improbable, many times more improbable than the most farfetched naturalistic explanation of the data, then it might be reasonable to accept an otherwise very implausible naturalistic explanation. But there seems to be no argument to show that miracles are tremendously improbable. It is not enough to say that they are rare and unusual—and event may be rare and unusual but still to be expected in given circumstances. It is rare to have world records in athletic events broken, but it is to be expected at the Olympic Games. President Ford's pardon of ex-President Nixon was a rare and unusual event, but not unexpected in the very unusual circumstances which then prevailed. The Resurrection of Christ was a rare and unusual event, but in the context of His life and teaching, was it unexpected?

It is even possible to give some general idea of the circumstances in which miracles are to be expected. The first is extraordinary goodness or holiness on the part of the miracle worker. As the man born blind said to the Jews, "We know for certain that God does not answer the prayers of sinners." The second circumstance is the need to back up or authenticate a message from God. Christ was as good and holy the year before He began his public ministry as He was after He began it, but He did not begin to work miracles until He began to preach. There is, I think, a third condition: an openness and willingness to learn on the part of the audience. In some places Christ worked few miracles because of the hardness of heart of those in that place. Christ worked no miracles at Herod's request; He cast none of His pearls before that swine.

Let me pause here and make a parenthetical remark which is not directly relevant to my main theme, but has a connection with it. I have been mentioning as examples various miracles attributed to Christ in the Gospels, including the Fourth Gospel. This may seem to some to fly in the face of much recent biblical scholarship, which has argued that the miracles attributed to Christ are additions to the record of His life made by later generations of Christian believers rather than accounts of what actually happened at the time given by eyewitnesses. Now in some cases there may be reasons for doubting on purely textual grounds whether a certain part of the New Testament as we now have it was part of the original record, for example, in the debated case of the "long ending" of Mark's Gospel. But a careful examination of a good deal of "higher" criticism (as opposed to textual criticism) of the New Testament shows that it is not the case that the miraculous element is rejected because the text is doubtful, but rather that the text is regarded as doubtful because of a prior rejection of any miraculous element.

Insofar, then, as we can show by philosophical argument that neither science nor reason requires us to reject the possibility of miracles, we undermine the kind of doubt as to the reliability of our texts which is based on hostility to a miraculous or supernatural element in Scripture. We must entertain the possibility that Luke recounts the Virgin birth of Christ because it actually happened and not because the later Christian community borrowed elements from pagan mythology to enhance the importance of the founder of Christianity. To the unbiased eye the first hypothesis might seem much more plausible than the second. We might even be daring enough to entertain the hypothesis that the Fourth Gospel, which is full of eyewitness detail and local knowledge, was actually written by the Apostle John, and that its theological depth as compared to the other Gospels is due to the fact that John understood his Master better than some of the other disciples, rather than due to later interpretations by second-generation Christians. Plato's picture of Socrates is more profound than Xenophon's, at least partly because Plato was better fitted to understand Socrates than Xenophon was.

Do historical arguments based on the New Testament record, which argue that miracle is the only or best explanation of certain well-attested events amount to a *proof* that miracles have occurred? So long as we understand that the term "proof" means something different in historical studies than it does in mathematics or science or philosophy, it may well be that we do have adequate historical proof of miracles. But to show this in detail would involve getting down to the historical nitty-gritty, and I cannot do that here.

Let me turn, then, to the related question of what miracles prove. If it is granted, at least for the sake of argument, that God exists, that miracles are possible, and that we have good historical evidence that miracles marked the beginning of Christianity, does this prove the Christian claim to the truth of the revelation given to us by Christ? Before we can decide this, we will have to examine three apparent difficulties.

The first difficulty is what we might call the problem of contradictory miracles. If it were the case that genuine miracles were worked in support of contradictory religious revelations, we would not know what to think. It would be like a witness whose integrity we were absolutely sure of giving contradictory testimony for both sides of a dispute. Something would have to give. We would have to conceive that the witness was not really honest, or deny that he actually gave the testimony on both sides, or find some way of showing that the contradiction was only apparent.

Similarly, if it were claimed that miracles are worked in support of contradictory religious revelations, we would have to give up the idea of miracles as proving a system of religion, unless we could show that the contradiction was only apparent, or that one set of opposed miracles was not genuine.

In some cases perhaps we can show that there is no genuine conflict. Many religious believers accept both Old Testament and New Testament miracles, and deny the claim (which has been made) that Old Testament miracles worked in the name of the One God of Judaism are in some ways incompatible with New Testament miracles worked in the name of God the Father, God the Son, and God the Holy Spirit. (This is, of course, because they would deny, on theological grounds, that Christian belief in the Trinity amounts to belief in three Gods.)

Many Christian religious believers would not even deny the possibility that God might have worked miracles for the "virtuous pagans" before Christ, to encourage them to emphasize those parts of their religion closest to the truth. If, for instance, God had worked a miracle for the Egyptian Pharaoh Amenhotep in support of his efforts to establish monotheism and overthrow the dark gods of old Egypt, they would find in this no challenge to Christianity, even though Amenhotep's monotheism might have been very crude and contained elements of untruth.

What would threaten the argument from miracles for the truth of Christianity would be genuine miracles worked in opposition to Christian claims or in support of incompatible claims. If, for instance, a Moslem holy man raised a man from the dead in order to persuade Christians that Mohammed's revelation had superseded that of Christ, this would be a case of genuine incompatibility. However, so far from any case of this kind being established, it is hard to show that any case of this kind has even been claimed. General statements are often made by opponents of Christianity that miracles are claimed by all religions, but leading cases of these alleged claims are hard to come by.

Certainly fairy-tale-like legends sometimes grow up around a figure like Buddha or Mohammed, but these have certain common characteristics. Such tales arise centuries after the time of their alleged occurrence. They contain strong elements of the fantastic (e.g., Mohammed riding his horse to the moon) and in their manner of telling they reveal their kinship to legend and myth. Compare any of these accounts with the accounts we find in the Gospels and the difference in atmosphere is at once apparent. Either the Gospel accounts are eyewitness accounts of real events occurring in genuine places, or the four writers we call Matthew, Mark, Luke, and John independently invented, out of the clear blue sky, a sort of realistic fantasy or science fiction which has no antecedents and no parallels in ancient literature. Those who have no metaphysical objections to miracles may find the hypothesis that the events really happened as they are related immensely more plausible than the other hypothesis.

It may be worthwhile to take a quick look, for purposes of comparison, at the closest thing we have around the time of the Gospels to an attempt at a realistic fantasy. This is the story of Appollonius of Tyana, written about A.D. 220 by Flavius Philostratus, which is sometimes referred to by controversialists as if it were a serious rival to the Gospel accounts of Christ's ministry and miracles. Penguin Classics publishes an excellent little paper back edition of this story, to which you may go for details, but let me note a few points in passing.

The story concerns a wandering sage who allegedly lived from the early years of the first century until about A.D. 96 or 98. Philostratus mentions some earlier sources for his work but at least some of these sources are probably his own invention. For one thing, Philostratus's account contains serious historical inaccuracies about things like dates of rulers, which seem to rule out reliance on any early source. The work was later used as anti-Christian propaganda, to discredit the uniqueness of Christ's miracles by setting up a rival miracle worker, as Socrates was sometimes set up as a rival to Chirst as a martyr and teacher of virtue.

Still, there is some evidence that a neo-Pythagorean sage named Apollonius may really have lived, and thus Philostratus's work is a real example of what some have thought the Gospels to be: a fictionalized account of the life of a real sage and teacher, introducing miraculous events to build up the prestige of the central figure. It thus gives us a good look at what a real example of a fictionalized biography would look like, written at a time and place not too far removed from those in which the Gospels were written.

The first thing we notice is the fairy-tale atmosphere. There is a rather nice little vampire story, which inspired a minor poem by Keats, entitled *Lamia*. There are animal stories about, for instance, snakes in India big enough to drag off and eat an elephant. The sage wanders from country to country and wherever he goes he is likely to be entertained by the king or emperor, who holds long conversations with him and sends him on his way with camels and precious stones.

Interspersed with picturesque adventures there are occasional accounts of miracles, often involving prophecy or mind reading. A ruffian threatens to cut Apollonius's head off and the sage laughs and shouts out the name of a day three days hence; on that day the ruffian is executed for treason. Here is a typical passage about healing miracles:

> There came a man about thirty who was an expert lion-hunter but had been attacked by a lion and dislocated his hip, and so was lame in one leg. But the Wise Man massaged his hip and this restored the man to an upright walk. Someone else who had gone blind went away with his sight fully restored, and another man with a paralysed arm left strong again. A woman too, who had had seven miscarriages was cured through the prayers of her husband as follows. The Wise Man told the husband, when his wife was in labor, to bring a live rabbit under his cloak to the place where she was, walk around her and immediately release the hare: for she would lose her womb as well as the baby if the hare was not immediately driven away (Bk. 3, Sec. 39).

Now the point is not that Apollonius is no serious rival to Christ; no one ever thought he was except perhaps a few anti-Christian polemicists about the time of some of the early persecutions of the Church. The point is that this is what you get when imagination goes to work on a historical figure in classical antiquity; you get miracle stories a little like those in the Gospels, but also snakes big enough to eat elephants, kings and emperors as supporting cast, travelers' tales, ghosts, and vampires. Once the boundaries of fact are crossed we wander into fairyland. And very nice, too, for amusement or recreation. But the Gospels are set firmly in the real Palestine of the first century, and the little details are not picturesque inventions but the real details that only an eyewitness or a skilled realistic novelist can give.

As against this, those who wish to eliminate miracles from the Gospels have not textual evidence, but theories. We do not have any trace of early sober narratives of the life of Christ without miracles and later versions in which miracles are added. What we have is a story with miracles woven into its very texture. Someone once made a shrewd point about this. Christ, say the Gospels, "went about doing good." Fine. But what good did He do? Did He clothe the naked, visit prisoners, counsel people on personal problems? No. He went about making the extravagant claim to forgive sins and backing this up by working miracles, mostly miracles of healing. Eliminate this element and, setting aside His preaching, what good did He go about doing?

The point is that the miraculous is interwoven with the primary story of Christianity in a way in which the miraculous is not interwoven with the primary story of Buddhism or Mohammedanism. Again, however, this is a matter for detailed inquiry into comparative religion and the history of religions.

The second major difficulty as to the evidential value of miracles which we will consider is the objection that what seems to us to be an exception to the natural order may just be the operation of some natural regularities which we do not yet understand. Perhaps, says this objection, Jesus was merely a rare type of charismatic personality who could arouse a faith response in people such that their minds acted on their bodies in a way that freed them from illness. After all, the relation of the mind and body in illness is a mysterious one, and some studies suggest that mental attitude has a great deal to do with illness. Thus we may some-day understand scientifically, and even be able to reproduce, some of Christ's apparently miraculous cures.

The first comment to make on this line of objection is that, like any argument which depends on what science *may* be able to discover in the future, it is extremely weak. But we can also ask what range of illnesses and cures this theory is supposed to account for. For example, Christ might have cured a paralytic because the paralysis was hysterical and subject to psychosomatic healing. But what about the cure of leprosy? What about the cure of the man blind from birth? And it is no use saying that psychosomatic illnesses cured by the impact of a charismatic per-sonality account for *some* of Christ's cures and that the rest are fictional, for this would be to pick and choose among the evidence in a blatant way. If I am allowed to pick which of the evidence I will explain and reject the rest, I can make almost any theory look plausible.

But, of course, the cases which are decisive against any theory of psychosomatic cures are the raisings from the dead reported in all four Gospels. A last-ditch attempt to explain these "naturally" might be to allege that the seemingly dead persons were only in a cataleptic state, but cases of this kind are so rare that to allege this as an explanation of the raising of the daughter of the Jairus, *and* of the son of the widow of Nain, *and* Lazarus, brings in coincidence to a fantastic degree. Each of these accounts is highly circumstantial, and none can be plausibly treated as a variation on one of the others.

In others words, the proponent of the view that Christ's cures were psychosomatic—"faith healing" in a limiting sense—must make up his mind whether or not he accepts the written records as factual or fic-tional, or whether he holds them to be a mixture of fact and fiction. If the records are fictional, no explanation of the cures is necessary. If the account is factual, all of the reported miracles must be accounted for, not just those which can be plausibly accounted for on naturalistic grounds. If it is alleged that there is a mixture of fact and fiction, there must be an independent standard of what is factual in the record and what is fictional. We cannot in logic allow the principle of choice: "What

I can explain is fact, the rest is fiction." (Think what ex-President Nixon could have done to the Watergate story using that principle!)

If the proponent of an explanation by so far unknown laws of nature goes so far as to say that even raisings from the dead can be accounted for by these laws, he must again explain a tremendous implausibility: either that these laws operated coincidentally in the neighborhood of Jesus, or that an obscure provincial carpenter somehow was able to discover and make use of natural powers and possibilities that none of the wise sages or deep researchers had ever been able to master or control.

A final difficulty about the evidential value of miracles rests on the fear that some supernatural power less than that of God might account for the wonders worked by Christ—that Jesus did His works, if not by the powers of Beelzebub, then at least by the power of some spiritual being less than God. To say what power this might be, of course, would be in some sense to give a theological account of what powers greater than human there might be, and how they are related to one another.

Consider, however, a line of argument sometimes heard from people influenced by certain sorts of Eastern religions, which goes something like this: Yes, of course Jesus was able to do apparently miraculous things; He was a Master, or Adept, and they can all do things of this sort. Jesus, living at the time and place that He did, tried to teach the Palestinian people a simple religion of love, put in terms of their own religious concepts, and this message has reached us in a distorted form. His real power lay in spiritual enlightenment, which you can learn by practicing Yoga (*or* going to Tibet, *or* studying with Mahatma X, or the like).

Again, there is a large blank check, drawn this time not on science, but on some sort of mystical religion. A friend of mine, arguing religion with opponents who seemed dogmatically sure of what God could or could not create, would challenge them, if they knew so much about creation, to create just one small rabbit—"to establish confidence." A similar challenge might be put to the exponents of "Eastern Wisdom" to duplicate even the least of Christ's miracles, to establish their claims. If they admit their own lack of power but claim others have performed some feats as great as Christ's, the problem simply reduces to one of the evidence for rival miracles discussed earlier.

In addition, there is a theological question as to whether a wise and loving God would allow people to be misled by permitting some lesser being to work apparent miracles. Real raising from the dead, creation of food or wine which is genuine and not illusory—such miracles seem by their nature to be the province of God only. But even if such things as the reading of thoughts or the manipulation of matter in scientifically inexplicable ways were possible to powers less than God, would God permit such occurrences in a context which gave rise to a false belief in men of good will, or seriously challenged the true beliefs of those already on the right path? A priori, it would seem not; and again, it does not seem that there is any reliable record of any such occurrences. (This is not to say that God may not sometimes permit "wonders" of this sort to be worked in order to refute them by His own power—for example, the story in Acts of the girl with the "prophetic spirit.")

The preceding comments, necessarily brief, give some indication of the lines along which the evidential value of miracles must be assessed. Are there indeed rival miracles? Can miracles be explained as due to powers less than God? If the answer to all these questions is no, then we are forced to grant that miracles give a strong argument for the existence of God.

DISCUSSION QUESTIONS

1. If you are a religious believer, do you believe that miracles occur? Why or why not?
2. If you are not a religious believer, how would you account for apparent miracles?
3. Is there a contradiction between accepting a scientific world-view and believing in miracles? (Be sure to define your terms.)
4. What assumptions are necessary before we can even make sense of the idea of a miracle?
5. What views of the universe are incompatible with a belief in miracles? Do these views have any drawbacks?
6. Are there any historical events which it seems plausible to regard as miraculous? If not, why not? If so, which ones and why?
7. Could a seemingly miraculous event give us grounds for believing in God? Why or why not?
8. Have contradictory miracles (in the sense discussed in this chapter) ever occurred? Defend your answer.
9. Could the events in the miracle stories of the Old and New Testaments be explained scientifically? Why or why not?
10. Could some miracles be worked only by God, not by some lesser superhuman power? Why or why not?

SUGGESTED READINGS

BRODY, BARUCH, ed., *Readings in the Philosophy of Religion.* Englewood Cliffs,
    N.J.: Prentice-Hall, Inc., 1974:
    DIETL, PAUL J., "On Miracles," pp. 413–71.
    HOLLAND, R. L., "The Miraculous," pp. 458–63.
    HUME, DAVID, "Skeptical Challenge to the Belief in Miracles," pp.
        437–42.
    NOWELL-SMITH, PATRICK, "Miracles," pp 440–50.
HICK, JOHN H., *Philosophy of Religion,* 2d ed. Englewood Cliffs, N.J.: Prentice-
    Hall, Inc., 1973:
    Chapter 2, "Grounds for Belief in God," pp. 29–30.

The Bible:

Myth or History?

6

Rabbi Benjamin Singer grinned ruefully as he saw Mrs. Day's portly form bearing down on him. An earnest lady—very. But at least she was interested in talking seriously about religion, not just exchanging empty generalities like most people at these Interfaith Coffee Hours. But he wished she wouldn't always ask him about "the Jewish position" on this, that, or the other. He was rather tired of explaining the differences between Orthodox Judaism and a Reform temple such as his own, and then trying to do justice to the differences within his own congregation. She had evidently taken some of this in, though, for this time she began, "Rabbi Singer, I would like to know what *you* think about these new theories about the Bible. Reverend Andrews gave a *very* disturbing sermon last Sunday. It really seems that many ministers don't believe in the historical truth of the Bible any more. Surely you don't feel that way?"

This was a new tack for Mrs. Day and Singer tried to give her as good an answer as he could on the spur of the moment. "Well, of course as a Jew I'm not concerned with the historical accuracy of some parts of your Bible. I could hardly accept the more traditional views of your Gospel and still retain my present religious beliefs. But I can say something about my approach to the Torah—what you would call the Old Testament. It is a collection of books which contain all sorts of things—some very great religious poetry, reams of very technical legal regulations, some mythical stories which have no historical purpose but rather a moral or didactic purpose—like, for instance, the story of Jonah. There *is* some writing in this collection of books which is historical in intent—for example, the whole cycle of stories about King David. But some of these "historical" writings are very different indeed from what we moderns would think of as history. They are history turned to myth or something midway between myth and history. I think that these parts of Scripture are no worse for that; they shouldn't be blamed for not achieving something which they aren't trying to achieve."

Mrs. Day was dubious. "Yes, I see that, but would you say they were *just* myths?"

How could he explain this without getting too technical? Ben wondered. Well, he could try.

"The major advance in Scriptural studies lately has been what's called 'form criticism': trying to find out what literary form is being used in a given book or even in a given passage and then judging the book or passage in terms of what we can expect from that literary form. You don't expect parables to be history; you don't expect mythologized history to be modern scientific history. For a Jew, the story of his people as recorded in what you would call the Old Testament is vitally important to his religion, to his very identity as a Jew. But to have this importance it need not be regarded as literal historical truth."

"But, Rabbi Singer, isn't there a point beyond which this kind of acceptance of a mythological element can't go?" asked Mrs. Day. "I mean, you can accept some of the details of the story of Moses as mythological perhaps, but surely for most Jewish people the statement that God brought Israel out of Egypt must express a truth which can't be reduced to just a story about the migration of a Middle Eastern people. Take Moses himself; legendary stories may have clustered around the figure of Moses, but if you reduce Moses himself to a myth you've surely destroyed something vital to Jewish belief."

Singer nodded. There was a brain behind Mrs. Day's clubwoman appearance. He tried to answer honestly. "Well, I'd say so myself, but then I'm moderately conservative in these matters. Some liberal Jews would be quite happy to make Moses a myth: just an expression of certain ideals of the Jewish people."

Mrs. Day leaned forward earnestly. "That's just what Reverend Andrews said. He said that Christian theologians make a distinction between the 'Christ of faith' and the 'historical Jesus,' and the Jewish theologians could make a distinction between Moses as a faith figure in the Jewish belief system and the historical Moses—even if there was indeed a single leader of that name at that period of history. He said that the question of whether Moses plays a certain role in the Jewish belief system is quite different from any historical question, and answering a historical question doesn't answer the question of Moses' place in Jewish belief."

Singer answered her with a slight hesitation. "I don't want to put down people who hold that kind of theory, but I must disagree. They distinguish a historical question and a question of religious belief, which is all right, though possibly misleading. They say that answering the historical question doesn't answer the question of belief, which again is all right if properly understood. But then they go on to say, it would seem, that the historical question is *irrelevant* to the question of belief, and that's highly questionable: It certainly doesn't follow from the previous statements at any rate.

"The historical question is whether there was a Jewish leader who was brought up at the Egyptian court, killed an Egyptian and fled, returned and led the Jewish people out of exile, and so forth. The question of belief is whether Moses is to be regarded as a prophet sent by God to lead the Jewish people out of bondage. But the question of belief presupposes the historical account and depends on it. If Moses *didn't* lead the children of Israel out of Egypt, then that in itself answers the question as to whether God sent him to lead them out of Egypt."

Ben could see that Mrs. Day was pleased by his answer, but still worried by what her minister had said. She replied a little uncertainly, "Well, Reverend Andrews said that the important thing about the Jewish belief is that *God* delivered their people from Egypt; whether He did it through a particular person with a particular history is unimportant."

Singer was getting a little impatient with Andrews's opinions —Heaven knew the man was no great scholar. He said, a bit dogmatically, "Jewish belief is not only that God delivered them from Egypt but that He did so in a particular way, through a particular human being, Moses, who therefore deserves a certain kind of respect and honor. And it was just Moses himself who saw the burning bush and saw God on Mount Sinai; the people as a whole saw only what God accomplished *through* Moses. You can't subtract Moses as a historical figure and still have the story as it's traditionally understood. And, because a question isn't *just* historical doesn't mean it has no historical element at all."

Ben glanced at his watch—he'd have to go in a minute. Had he overstated his case? Perhaps he should qualify what he had said a little. "I'm really somewhere in the middle on the question, Mrs. Day. There are Orthodox Jews who take a much more literalistic view than I do, and there are Jewish scholars who take a view very much like Dr. Andrews's. But I think that a great many Jews are just as disturbed by the idea of giving up the historical Moses as you are by the idea of giving up a historical Jesus."

Mrs. Day had seen him glance at his watch and said, "I see you have to leave, Rabbi. But it's always interesting to talk to you. I'm so glad to have heard the Jewish position." But she gave a little smile, almost a grin, as she said the last words, and Ben was smiling too as he moved toward the door. Always a mistake to judge by appearances. He had never suspected Mrs. Day of having a sense of humor.

The situation pictured in this story is a familiar one in many Jewish and Christian religious groups today. Many religious scholars and leaders, many rabbis, ministers, and priests have become convinced that they must reject traditional interpretations of the Scriptures and reinterpret the basic documents of their faith in a radically new way. Often at least part of their motive in making these radical reinterpretations is the conviction that present-day religious believers will not accept traditional interpretations. But many lay people are shocked or dismayed by the radical reinterpretations they hear from the pulpit, as Mrs. Day was in our story. Some of them turn to more traditional interpreters, and as a result more traditional and orthodox forms of Christianity and Judaism have recently shown greater growth and more stability than more "liberal" forms of these faiths. Other lay people are merely confused or worried by the new ideas, and as a result some drift away from religious practice.

It is sometimes claimed that historians simply as historians regard Old and New Testament history as unreliable on some independent historical grounds. But actually the situation is far more complex than this. Many events which are regarded as firmly established historically have far less documentary evidence than many biblical events, and the documents on which historians rely for much secular history are written much longer after the event than many records of biblical events. Furthermore we have many more copies of biblical narratives than of secular histories, and the surviving copies are much earlier than those on which our evidence for secular history is based. If the biblical narratives did not contain accounts of miraculous events or have reference to God, angels, etc., biblical history would probably be regarded as much more firmly established than most of the history of, say, Classical Greece and Rome.

But because the biblical accounts do mention miracles and do involve reference to God, to angels and demons, etc., considerations other than purely historical ones come into the picture. Some historians are convinced as part of their general world-view that miracles don't happen and that there is no spiritual world. Other historians try to avoid prejudging such philosophical and religious issues and to present a neutral account of history which leaves open the question of whether such events occur. Even historians who are religious believers often try to present history in a neutral or "objective" fashion because they do not want to seem to impose their religious beliefs on others. Thus whether biblical history is good history is not merely a technical question.

While we cannot do full justice to this controversy, we will try in this chapter to give some of the pros and cons of a more traditional or liberal interpretation of the Jewish and Christian Scriptures as opposed to the more "liberal" or "modernistic" interpretations. One area of controversy is between those who take the traditional view that the miracle stories of the Old and New Testaments are literally true, and those who defend a "demythologizing," "secularizing" interpretation of the Scriptures: the view that we must reinterpret stories about intervention by God in the physical universe as being really about changes in the minds and hearts of human beings.

Those who wish to "demythologize" Scripture reject *particular* accounts of miracles in Scripture because they hold a *general* view about the meaning of miracle stories, which in turn is based on a general view about Scriptual interpretation, part of which is the view that Ben Singer mentioned in our story, a form-critical approach to Scripture. In their view, many elements in the supposedly historical accounts in the Old and New Testaments are really mythological. The account in Exodus of the plagues of Egypt, for example, seems to them to have the form of a folk-talk or fairy story. The fact that there are ten plagues—one of the traditional "mystical numbers"—Moses' repeated returns to the Pharaoh, and the Pharaoh's repeated refusals to let the Jewish people go all seem to resemble traditional fairy tales, as do the "plagues." Water turning to blood and frogs raining down seem to be scientific impossibilities. Proponents of the myth argument would make similar claims about the central miracle story in the Gospels—Christ's Resurrection. In their view the Resurrection was not a historical event—not an intervention of God in the physical universe. Instead it was something that happened in the minds and hearts of Christ's followers. Some of their reasons for saying this are the same kinds of reasons that operate in their similar position about the Old Testament stories. Again there is what might be called fairy-tale atmosphere. Three days in the tomb—again, one of the "mystic numbers." Sudden magical appearances and vanishings in the post-Resurrection appearances. The seeming physical impossibility of revitalizing a corpse. But they cite two further reasons—inconsistency in the stories themselves, and the religious irrelevance of mere physical resurrection.

The traditionalist is unlikely to be impressed by the first point, the resemblance of Scriptural accounts to folk tales or fairy stories. He would point out that real events occur in groups of ten or within three days and we don't discredit stories about them on these grounds. Again, that we tell stories about magical appearances or disappearances or about water changing to blood or wine doesn't in itself show these things can't happen; we constantly write fiction about things which *do* happen, like faithful or unfaithful lovers, jealousy, battle, escapes.

The demythologizer might reply that changing water into wine or raising people from the dead occurs *only* in legends, not in scientific, verifiable history. That seems to the traditionalist to beg the question. If we are trying to decide whether certain events and miracles are historical or not, we can't have as a premise "Miracles don't occur in history" without arguing in a circle.

In reply, the demythologizer may claim that a scientific outlook, a belief that nature is governed by laws, is incompatible with a belief in miracles. But the traditionalist will rejoin that he can believe in scientific laws quite as much as anyone else. The difference is that in his view the laws are regularities imposed on nature by a personal being, who can therefore suspend the laws if he likes. Another possible view, which is sometimes identified with "*the* scientific view," is the view that the regularities we discover are somehow inherent in the nature of matter. Both views seem compatible with science. The issue between these two views is a philosophical one, not a scientific one.

At this stage we must make a distinction between the importance of miracle stories for Judaism and for Christianity. Judaism is a faith based on the historical experiences of a people, and for more Orthodox and conservative Jews these experiences include things, such as the story of the Exodus from Egypt, which embody miraculous elements. But these elements are not essential to Judaism in quite the same way that the Resurrection and the other miracles of Christ are essential to traditional Christianity. St. Paul's words in the fifteenth chapter of his first letter to the Corinthians, "If Christ has not risen, all your faith is delusion," would be echoed by most traditional Christians: To eliminate the miraculous element from Christianity is to make it different from what was traditionally thought of as Christianity, to change it more than the elimination of the miraculous element from Judaism would change Judaism.

Of course "liberal" Christians think that it is necessary to change traditional Christianity in just this way. They would claim that a faith which depended on miracles would be religiously unsatisfactory, completely naive, not a religion which modern man could accept. The Christian traditionalist might argue, however, that this "unsatisfactory, naive" faith was precisely the faith of the early Church, of St. Paul and the other apostolic writers and evangelists, and was based on the teachings of Christ Himself. He would cite Christ's constant appeal to his "works," which are in the context plainly his miracles, as evidence for his claims. He would cite St. Paul's passage from Corinthians mentioned above.

In reply to this the demythologizer might claim as a first principle of modern New Testament criticism that the miracle stories, the appeals to miracles, and so on were not in the original accounts of the life of Christ but were inserted by the early church as the mythologizing of the story began with the assimilation of Hellenic elements into the church. He might go on to argue on textual grounds that St. Paul is not referring to a physical resurrection. He would point out that St. Paul never refers to the empty tomb and seems to make no distinction between the immediately post-Resurrection appearances and Christ's appearance to Paul himself on the road to Damascus.

The traditionalist, however, could reply that the whole line of argument about insertion of elements in the Gospel story by the early church depends on there being enough time for this to happen. The original demythologizers specifically allowed several generations to pass before this insertion of mythological elements; they granted that it could not plausibly be claimed to have occurred while eyewitnesses to Jesus' life were alive. But our latest dates for the composition of the Gospels have been pushed back and back on purely textual grounds; we have a time span which many of the original demythologizers would have granted was not adequate for the mythologizing to occur. We also have the evidence of the Pauline epistles. There is no serious doubt that those epistles were composed within the lifetime of eyewitnesses to the events of Christ's life. Now if you grant mythological elements in Paul, then these are right back in the time period when the insertion of such elements is least plausible, according to the original demythologizing theories.

Another argument used by demythologizers is the argument from apparent contradictions in the Scriptures. The traditionalist would deny that there are any logical inconsistencies with known facts or any logical contradictions between different statements in the Scriptures, while he might grant that there are some statements that are *hard* to reconcile with fact or *hard* to reconcile with each other.

It may be illuminating to consider some specific charges of inconsistency made by the demythologizer and consider some possible answers to these charges from the point of view of traditional Christianity. Of course, even if the charges of inconsistency can be successfully refuted, this does not prove that the traditional view is true, but it would remove an important stumbling block in the way of accepting that view.

One such charge is a charge of inconsistency with known facts. Some Scripture scholars claim to find in the teachings of Jesus and the belief of the early Church a belief that the world would come to an end within the lifetime of the first followers of Jesus.

To this the traditional Christian would reply that in order to make a case that Christ or the early Church expected an immediate end to the world, you have to pick and choose your evidence very selectively, ignoring evidence on the other side. The traditionalist argues that this is just what the demythologizers have done to get their picture of an "apocolyptic Christ," a Christ who taught that the world would soon end. If you actually look at the documents, the picture is much more confusing. Whenever Christ was asked a straight question about when the world would end, He said very strongly that no one, not even He Himself, knew when it would end. He did, however, make certain statements about the future in which the fall of Jerusalem and the end of the world seem to be intermingled in a way which is rather puzzling. He then seems to say that "these things" or "all these things" will happen within the lifetime of people listening to Him. The destruction of Jerusalem by the Romans did indeed occur within their lifetime. But there seems to be no record of early Christians being disappointed or disillusioned because the world hadn't ended and, even more impressively, no evidence that the early anti-Christian propagandists thought of this as an argument against Christian belief. The enemies of the early Church used every argument they could find against Christianity, but there is no record of anyone saying in effect, "Aha, you fools expected the world to end within the lifetime of your first members; here they are all dead and the world hasn't ended!" Historically, every time a sect or group within Christianity has falsely predicted the end of the world at a certain time, you find the group breaking up in disillusionment when it doesn't happen and opponents of the group throwing up their foolishness to them. There is no record of that happening in early Christianity.

Another kind of charge is the charge of internal inconsistency— the claim that statements made in different Gospels or even within a single Gospel, contradict one another. The traditionalist in fact wishes to argue that the best explanation of the total evidence given in the Gospels—the empty tomb, the post-Resurrection appearances, the effect on the early Church, and so on—is that Christ actually and physically rose from the dead. But on particular points where the evidence seems to be in conflict it seems that all that the traditionalist can reasonably be asked to do is give at least one plausible way of explaining away the apparent contradiction. The burden of proof is on the traditionalist to show that resurrection rather than hallucination or deceit is the most plausible explanation of the known facts. But if the demythologizers try to answer him by citing apparent contradictions in the evidence, the burden of proof is on them to show that they really are contradictions. All the traditionalist has to do is show that they *can* be explained away, not that a particular explanation of them is highly probable in isolation from the evidence as a whole.

Some difficulties cited by the demythologizers are the number of angels at the tomb, whether the women did or did not tell the Apostles what they had seen, whether the stone was rolled away by an angel or found rolled away.

The traditionalist, to explain these things, may ask his opponent to grant two principles of New Testament interpretation. The first is that something which is not mentioned is not thereby denied, and the second, which is a sort of corollary of the first, is that when something is described right after something else, it doesn't mean that it followed the thing first described immediately. The Gospels are often written rather naively, like a child's story where everything is strung together with "and". "We went to the zoo and we saw the lions and we had lunch and we rode the merry-go-round and we came home. . . ."

When a story is told in this way a considerable time may elapse between two incidents run together by this kind of telling, and just as in the child's story about the zoo, some events may be omitted and have to be supplied by someone else. For example, the parent who took the children to the zoo may tell the other parent, "The children forgot to tell you that. . . ." The traditionalist often argues that the differences in detail in the four Gospels are just what we would expect of a true story told by several different witnesses.

In defense of this view the traditionalist can offer a conjectural timetable which gives one way of resolving the apparent contradictions. Begin at first light on Easter morning. Before that the women could not see to go to the tomb, and Jerusalem very likely had city gates which were locked until first light. In one view, at first light *two* groups of women set out, one from Bethany, where Christ and the Apostles had been staying, and one group from Jerusalem, where some of the women almost certainly lived. They set out by prearrangement to meet at the tomb and embalm the body of Christ. At first light also the stone is rolled away and the soldiers in the guard are struck with terror. Matthews' Gospel makes it sound as if this happened when the women were already there, but it is very likely that they were not and that the source of this part of the story is one of the guards. Granted the truth of the story, nothing is likelier than that some of the guards became Christians. (We are here using the second principle: The fact that Matthew describes the angel speaking to the women just after he describes the rolling away of the stone doesn't mean it happened just after. Or we could apply the first principle directly: That Matthew doesn't mention a lapse of time between the two incidents doesn't mean there wasn't one, or that he means to deny a lapse of time.) The next thing that happens, in this reconstruction, is that the Jerusalem group of women, including Salome, arrive at the tomb, find the stone rolled away, enter the tomb, find a seated angel who tells them to give the message to the Jerusalem disciples to meet Jesus in Galilee. These women run away in fear and do not immediately tell anyone what they have seen.

This is essentially the account in Mark's Gospel. Mark also mentions Mary Magdalene and Mary the mother of James, but although he says all three set out for the tomb, he does *not* say they set out together. In this view, Mary Magdalene and Mary the mother of James, along with Joanna, leave from Bethany at first light and arrive at the tomb after the Salome party has left. The account in Matthew and Luke applies to this party. Luke says they saw two angels. Matthew mentions only one, but by our first principle this doesn't deny there were two. The messages given to the women in the Matthew and Luke accounts can easily be fitted together. "He is not here, He is risen as He told you; tell his disciples" is the essence of both messages. This group leaves, but Mary Magdalene, who is the youngest, goes more quickly, and she goes straight to Peter and John. The other women, returning more slowly and perhaps by an easier and less direct way, have the encounter with the risen Jesus described in Matthew; this group does tell the Apostles what they have seen, as Luke tells us.

Why does Mark give us the story of the Salome group rather than that of the other group? Traditionally the Cenacle, the house of the Last Supper, was Mark's family home. Some of the Jerusalem group must have been relatives or friends of his family. So he gives us *their* story rather than the story of the other group. The next thing which happens is that Peter comes to the tomb and finds it empty, as Luke tells us. John's Gospel essentially picks up at this point after telling us that Mary Magdalene (no mention of other women, but we can apply principle one) finds the tomb empty and the stone moved. No mention of angels, but by the same principle this does not deny their presence. John's Gospel tells us that John went with Peter—not mentioned by Luke but compatible with Luke's account. Both accounts mention finding the graveclothes. John's Gospel mentions something peculiar about them— that they were not unwound. Peter and John leave, and Mary Magdalene has that beautifully described meeting with Christ which is mentioned in passing in the "long ending" to Mark's Gospel.

These last verses of Mark are not in his usual style and contain words found nowhere else in Mark. There is some evidence that these words are an early credal formula which was added to Mark's Gospel either by Mark himself or almost immediately after the writing of his Gospel. There is good precedent for an author's ending a piece of writing with a creed or prayer used in the Church; St. Paul did it several times. If it was added, then it represents a tradition separate from Mark, but that strengthens the evidence for the Resurrection rather than weakening it. What about the copies of Mark's Gospel which lack this ending? The original Gospels were written on rolls of papyrus. Nothing is commoner than for a passage at the end of a work written on a papyrus roll to be lost by damage to the outside leaf of the roll.

We have gone through only the early history of the Resurrection appearances, but this covers the part where most demythologizers find alleged contradictions, and all the supposed inconsistencies mentioned have been given plausible solutions—the stone, the number of angels, whether the women reported what they saw. The traditionalist will claim that he tries to do justice to all the evidence in the record, whereas the demythologizers typically pick and choose, rejecting the evidence they don't like by labeling it a later addition or interpolation, but accepting details which help a particular theory. For instance, Mark's account of the rolling away of the stone by an angel says the "ground shook." Some critics reject the angel—he must be an interpolation—but accept the "ground shaking" as an earthquake which rolled away the stone. According to some theories, Christ's body fell into an earth crack which then closed up. This accounts for the rolled-away stone and the empty tomb. But it is obviously very implausible—a nice neat earthquake, which rolls away only one stone and makes one body disappear. And this approach operates by selecting evidence in a highly arbitrary way. If I say I met a man with green eyes who could read my mind, why take my word for the green eyes while calling me a liar about the mind reading?

The traditionalist goes on to argue that if you do not rule out miracle a priori, an actual resurrection is a much more plausible and likely account of the reported facts than any of the proposed "natural" explanations. If the tomb was not empty, why didn't the authorities produce the body? If it was empty, where was the body? If the Apostles stole it, why were they willing to face martyrdom for a lie? If something like an earthquake made it disappear, you need an independent explanation of why the Apostles believed they talked with and touched and ate with a risen Christ? And if it was hallucination, why would they have such an extraordinary hallucination? Why the extraordinary coincidence, as it would have to be, of a great moral teacher, an accidental disappearance of the body, and a climate for detailed and vivid hallucinations with no real parallel in history?

Another explanation of the recorded testimony given by some demythologizers is the gradual growth of a mythologized version of the Easter event in the minds of the first followers of Jesus. But if we are speaking of the first generation of believers, the traditionalist can challenge the plausibility of this view. Imagine what is being postulated in the case of, say, St. Peter. He has to know that as a matter of fact he never went to the tomb and found it empty, never spoke and ate with the risen Christ. Instead, he had some sort of inner experience of seeing that if you live in a certain way, a way as similar as possible to the way Christ lived, death doesn't matter, and sin can be overcome. But then, at some later stage, he comes to believe and preach something which is completely contrary to the experience he actually had. The human mind, the traditionalist claims, just doesn't work that way, especially in the case of all those who claimed to have seen the risen Christ. St. Paul, writing only about twenty years after the death of Christ, mentions an appearance of the risen Christ to five hundred people. If that was a myth or a metaphor, there would be plenty of people still alive who could challenge him. The traditionalist will conclude that the demythologizing view was plausible only when you could postulate several generations over which the mythology grew up. But paleographic evidence, radioactive dating of manuscript fragments, and so forth, has pushed the latest date for the Gospels back further and further. And there was never a great deal of doubt as to the authenticity of Paul's letters, which give us independent evidence about the Resurrection.

To the demythologizer, the traditionalist's whole approach to the New Testament is naive and old-fashioned. It cites particular sayings attributed to Christ as if we could safely take them as Christ's own words, uninterpreted by the Church, and particular incidents told in the Gospel accounts as if we could take them as actual historical events, not as stories told in a certain way for a certain religious purpose. But the traditionalist will reply that the reason he does these things is because he thinks that we do have at least the sense of Christ's own words (if not the exact words) and that the events recorded in the Gospels *are* actual historical events. He sees no incompatibility between their being actual historical events and their being told with a religious purpose, or grouped or organized in certain artificial ways. For example, in the late President Kennedy's *Profiles in Courage*, there are biographies of historical persons told for a particular moral and political purpose and incidents organized and selected in accordance with that purpose. But the events related are still historical events.

We have obviously only skimmed the surface of the debate between the demythologizer and the traditionalist. But perhaps we have said enough to show that there are arguments on both sides of the question and that it would be foolish for anyone to make up his mind on the issues without a careful examination of these arguments. And although the testimony of the experts must be taken into account, this is not a matter on which we can simply hand over our own judgment to the experts. We must consider the expert testimony, but we must then render our own verdict.

DISCUSSION QUESTIONS

1. What is your own view or interpretation of the Bible? How would you defend your view?

2. How would you judge a narrative which contained an account of a miracle? On what basis would you make your judgment?

3. How would the removal of the miraculous element from the Biblical stories, if this were possible, affect your own attitude toward these stories? Why?

4. Do you find any apparent inconsistencies in those parts of the Bible with which you are familiar? If so, what would you say about these inconsistencies? Why?

5. If someone were convinced of the historical truth of the Biblical accounts of Christ's Resurrection, how should this affect his attitude to religion? Why?

6. Can you cite any cases where a historical narrative had mythological elements added to it? What evidence do you have that this happened?

7. How long a period would be necessary for a historical event to become mythologized? What is the basis for your answer?

8. What arguments of the demythologizer or the traditionalist especially impressed you? Why?

9. What objection or addition would you like to make to what is said in this chapter?

10. What is the difference (if any) between the Bible and the holy books of other religions? Justify your answer.

SUGGESTED READINGS

HICK, JOHN, *Philosophy of Religion*. Englewood Cliffs, N.J.: Prentice-Hall, Inc., 1973.
    Chapter 4, "Revelation and Faith," pp. 48–67.
YANDELL, KEITH, *God, Man and Religion*. New York: McGraw-Hill Book Company, 1973:
    ALSTON, WILLIAM P., "Tillich's Conception of a Religious Symbol," pp. 252–61.
    DODD, C. H., "The Apostolic Preaching," pp. 55–61.
    FOY, MARVIN, "Tillich's Ontology and God," pp. 262–75.
    TILLICH, PAUL, "The Meaning and Justification of Religious Symbols," pp. 247–51.
YANDELL, KEITH, ed., *God, Man and Religion*. New York: McGraw-Hill Book Company, 1973:
    BULTMAN, RUDOLPH, "The Task of Demythologizing, pp. 191–201.
    HEPBURN, RONALD, "Demythologizing and the Problem of Validity," pp. 202–13.

Eastern Religion:

Wisdom from the East?

7

Ed Kelly shut his eyes for a minute hoping that what he saw would somehow go away, but when he opened them again he still saw the same thing. His son—his son the football player, his son the A student—sitting there in the Kellys' pleasant suburban living room, his head shaven and his mustard-colored robe clashing with the soft rose color of the newly reupholstered sofa. Ed tried to keep his voice calm, but it kept rising toward an almost hysterical note. "Tommy, what do you mean, you're a monk? I know the Church has changed, but monks don't go around dressed like that!"

Tom Kelly smiled at his father, that calm, rather indulgent smile which was making Ed so uneasy—it was so unlike any expression he had ever seen on his son's face. "Dad, I'm trying to put it in terms you'll understand. I'm not a Christian monk and certainly not a Roman Catholic monk. . . ." He paused, looking a little less calm, and Ed remembered that Tom had "left the Church" very dramatically last year when he had been dating that young divorced girl. That was typical of Tommy, Ed thought —Tom wasn't mad at the Church on his own behalf, but because he thought that the Church had messed up the girl's life. The girl was gone, but apparently Tom's anger at the Church was not.

But Tom was continuing, more slowly, "You see, Dad, I live at the ashram—what you migh call a monastery—and we have prayers and meditation together and share everything in common. We take it in turns to go out begging for money to support the place—that's what I'm supposed to be doing now." His father leaned forward and spoke earnestly: "Tommy, I don't care if you dress funny, I don't even care if you beg for money if it's for a good cause, but what is it all about? What does this group you belong to believe in?"

Tom was eager now, anxious to explain to his father. "Dad, remember when I was in Nam I tried to do as much traveling around the East as I could on my furloughs: Japan, Cambodia, Nepal. And remember how I got interested in Eastern religion? There's lots of different kinds of Buddhism and Hinduism, Dad, at least as many as there are denominations of Christianity. But just like the different denominations all have something in common, so we can call them all Christian, there's something in common among all these Eastern religions. And that's what our ashram is founded on, this wisdom that's common to all of the Eastern religions. We have guys who served in Viet Nam like me, and guys who belong to Asian ethnic groups and are trying to recover their heritage. . . ."

Ed brushed this aside for the moment. "Yes, Tommy, I see all that, but what is this wisdom of the East you're talking about?"

His son replied seriously, "It's not all that easy to express just in words, Dad, but I think that even you can see that some of the things we believe make real sense. Karma, for instance. You know how I always worried about the suffering in the world, not only people, but animals too." That was true. Ed knew: Tommy had been the kind of boy who ran errands for bedridden old ladies, and tried to cure birds with broken wings. Tom went on: "Karma explains that all living things are progressing towards God and that the suffering we have we deserve. . . ."

His father broke in harshly, "You think your mother deserved that cancer she had?"

Tom's voice was less calm than it had been as he replied, "Not in this life, Dad; you and I know what a saint she was. But in some previous life she had deserved to suffer, and by the wonderful way she accepted that suffering in this life she went up the scale; when she's born again, she'll be even closer to reaching her final goal."

Ed was still upset by the thought of his wife, who had died two years ago, and he snapped rather than said, "And what is this 'final goal?' "

Tom was calmer now that they had moved on to more theoretical ground. "You can call it God if you like, Dad, but it isn't personal. It's a state of peace and union where individual personalities vanish. Some religions call it Nirvana, some call it Nothingness. But it's the end of all trying and desiring."

Ed stood up now and looked at his son. "Tom, you're grown up now and you can do as you like. But remember, I was in the East, too, in *my* War. I've seen the people there not helping the sick or the starving because they deserved their suffering. We were both hurt a lot by the way your mother died, but I don't find your answers much consolation. If she's born again she doesn't know or remember us and we won't know or remember her if we're born again. And if the end of the whole business is to lose all personal identity, what's the use of all the suffering and trying anyway?" He saw that his words hadn't touched his son, that perhaps Tom hadn't even really listened, secure as he was in his new answer to life. An old quotation floated into Ed's mind. "East is East and West is West," he thought, and in Tom's case I wish to God they had never met.

There are bad ethnic jokes about all Orientals looking alike to Westerners, and now reverse ethnic jokes about all Westerners looking alike to Orientals. Both jokes contain a grain of truth; in a group of people or things strange to us we tend to notice common features rather than individual differences. This can be, and often is, a bad thing, but sometimes distance can lend perspective—from too close we often cannot see the wood for the trees. In this chapter I am going to have to make large generalizations about "Eastern Religion," and it is quite true that I will be ignoring important individual differences among Buddhism, Hinduism, Taoism, etc., and among different sects within each of these great Eastern religions. But though detailed knowledge is necessary for a full judgment, it is helpful for a preliminary appraisal to look at broad differences between Eastern religions and the Judeo-Christian tradition of the West. After making this broad contrast we will try to fit into the picture another great world religion, Islam.

We have used as our working definition of religion "belief in a God or gods" and in a "life after death," and it is on these two points that we can make our first major contrast. Western religions have traditionally seen God as personal and as sharply separate from the universe (the technical term for this is *transcedent*). Eastern religions in their popular form often have anthropomorphic gods, but at least in the more theoretical forms of Eastern religion the ultimate reality, what corresponds most closely to God in Western religions, is seen as impersonal. The issue of the transcendence of "God" in Eastern religion is more complex; many Eastern religions see the physical universe as unreal, a mere delusion, while what corresponds to God is seen as Reality. In these forms of religion separateness is an illusion; *all* that is ultimately real, including our own minds or souls, is *identical* with God. Thus we get the statement, "Everything that *exists* is God," with the qualification that illusion does not really exist.

Other Eastern religions seem to assert the formula, "Everything that exists is God," with less qualification, so that a tiger, a flower, a rock, are all in some sense God. The view that everything is God is called *pantheism*, and with some qualifications we can say that the tendency of Eastern religion is toward some form of pantheism, toward the idea that God is *immanent* (somehow in the universe) rather than *transcendent* (separate from the universe).

About life after death, the tendency of most Eastern religions has been to accept some form of the doctrine of *reincarnation* or *the transmigration of souls* in which the same person is born over and over again, leading a succession of human lives, or in some versions a succession of animal and human lives. Closely associated with the idea of reincarnation is the idea of *Karma*, or "cosmic justice," according to which what we enjoy or suffer in our present life is determined by our actions in previous lives.

With regard to the ethical code or moral point of view associated with Eastern religions, there is, as one might expect, considerable agreement with the Western religions. Parallels to the Ten Commandments and the Golden Rule—"Do to others as you would have them do to you" —can easily be found in the ethical teachings of Buddhism, Hinduism, Taoism, etc. But while Eastern religions agree with the Western religions on a day-to-day code of morality, there is a profound underlying difference in attitude, which can be seen in the following two quotations. The first is from the Hindu holy book *The Upanishads:*

> When all desires that cling to the heart disappear, then a mortal becomes immortal and even in this life attains liberation. . . . Into deep darkness fall all those who follow knowledge . . . the desire of children and wealth is the desire of the world. And this desire is vanity. . . . A man who knows that is not moved to grief or exultation on account of the evil or good he has done. He goes beyond both. What is done or left undone grieves him not.

The second is from a collection of Buddhist writings:

What then is the Holy Truth of Evil? Birth is evil, decay is evil, sickness is evil, death is evil. To be united with what one dislikes means suffering. To be separated from what one likes means suffering. In short all grasping . . . involves suffering.
What then is the Holy Truth of the Origin of Evil? It is . . . craving for sensuous experience, craving to perpetuate oneself [even] craving for extinction:
What then is the Holy Truth of the Stopping of Evil? It is the complete stopping of that craving, the withdrawal from it, the renouncing of it, throwing it back, liberation from it, nonattachment to it.

As can be seen in these two quotations, Hinduism and Buddhism agree (and this is true to some extent of other Eastern religions) on a certain diagnosis of human problems and a certain solution to them. The diagnosis is that desire for *anything* is the root of evil and the solution is to stop desiring anything. It is important to see the similarities of this view with certain ideas in the Western religious tradition, but also the basic differences. Some Christian spiritual writers have said things about the renunciation of desire which sound very much like the quotations we have just given, but two points have always been insisted on in the Western tradition. First, desire is not in itself bad; only misplaced or misdirected desire is. Second, a personal union with a personal God *is* to be desired, with all one's heart and mind and soul. Thus, a man or woman who gives up normal life to become a monk or nun or hermit believes that he or she is giving up things good in themselves—marriage, property, being part of the ordinary human society—for something better and more desirable—a personal union with God.

In contrast, the tendency of Buddhism especially is to regard desire itself as evil and to regard ordinary human life as at best "harmless," not making a person worse but certainly having no tendency to make a person better. Hinduism is less clear on this point, and there are passages in *The Upanishads* and elsewhere that sound much more like the Western view, that a personal union with God *should* be desired. But when one looks more closely at the Hindu ideas of the *atman,* or true self, and *Brahman,* the Supreme Reality, we again see basic differences from the Western view. In the last analysis, the atman is not really separate from Brahman, its separateness is an illusion we must overcome. And though Brahman can "manifest itself" as personal in the last analysis, the personhood of the Brahman is illusory too. In *The Upanishads* we find such statements as:

The Soul is Brahman, the Eternal.

This truth must be seen: there are not many, but only One.

Whereas in the Western tradition we have God creating souls separate from Himself, which are eventually united with Him while retaining their personal identity, in the Eastern tradition we have only one reality, Brahman, and the apparent separateness of the atman from Brahman is an illusion which must be overcome.

The perspective into which morality is put by this ultimate unity of atman and Brahman can be seen in the earlier quotations: In the long run the moral struggle too is illusory. For the "sage," or wise man, "what is done or left undone grieves him not"; he "is not moved to grief or exultation on account of the good or evil he has done." At most, wrong choices can increase the illusion of separateness and delay the eventual union of atman with Brahman. The apparent separation is unreal and can never be permanent. On the other hand, in the Western tradition damnation, ultimate separation from God, is possible. This creates moral problems as we saw in Chapter 2, but it does emphasize the real separateness of the soul and God in the Western view. The two are so separate that it is logically possible (though perhaps morally repugnant) that they should be eternally separate.

In this brief survey we have emphasized points of difference more than points of similarity between East and West, and we have tried to pick out some key differences between Eastern and Western approaches to religion. We have concentrated on Buddhism and Hinduism, since a great deal of the world's population accepts one or the other of these two religions, but much of what we have said applies to other Eastern religions such as Taoism, Sikhism, Jainism, etc. On the other hand, Islam, the great Near Eastern religion founded by Mohammed, is much more like the Western religions in most of the respects we have discussed. Islam believes in one personal God, Allah, hopes for a personal afterlife, and does not recommend doing away with desire.

Christianity and Islam are alike in being traced to an individual founder, but there are important differences. Mohammed saw himself merely as the last in a long line of prophets, among whom he numbered Christ as well as the Old Testament prophets. Within Christianity the claim was made (whether or not it was made by Christ Himself is disputed) that Jesus Christ was in some special sense the Son of God, and that he came not only to preach but also to suffer and die for the sins of the human race. Followers of Islam deny any such special status or mission to either Christ or Mohammed and see both merely as prophets, bearers of a message from God. Thus most followers of Islam object to the term "Mohammedan," which suggests that Mohammed occupies a position in Islam like that of Christ in Christianity. The correct terms are *Islam,* literally "submission to God," and *Moslem,* "one who submits to God."

The position of Prince Gautama, the Buddha, within Buddhism is different again. According to legend Gautama was an Indian prince whose parents tried to shield him from knowledge of suffering and death. Wandering away from his palace one day he met successively a man in the throes of a disease, a decrepit old man, and a funeral procession carrying a corpse. The shock of seeing these aspects of the human condition, having previously been unaware of them, led Gautama to renounce his possessions and wander over the countryside in search of wisdom. After many tribulations and much searching he sat down under a Bo tree and experienced "enlightenment," seeing the Holy Truths mentioned in our earlier quotation. (The title "Buddha" means "the enlightened one.") He then gathered disciples around him and began teaching the doctrine of liberation from desire which we have already discussed.

The probable dates for the death of Gautama are about 544 B.C., the traditional date, or around 483 B.C., the date now preferred by many scholars. But the first Buddhist scriptures that we have any knowledge of were compiled in Ceylon about the third century B.C., and the first written version which survives is from the first century A.D., five hundred years after the life and death of Gautama. However, this does not have the same importance for Buddhism as it would for Christianity or Islam, since it is not the life of Gautama which matters but the truths he taught. Indeed, the very nature of Buddhism, which teaches that the material world is illusory, makes unimportant the historical details of Gautama's life.

At least some forms of Buddhism teach that Gautama was not the only Buddha; the term is made a generic name for a human being who attains complete enlightenment, and there may have been many such persons in the course of history. Thus, unlike the terms "King Messiah" in traditional Judaism or "Christ" within Christianity, which necessarily refer only to one individual, "Buddha" is the name of a state rather than a person (as "Saint" is used in traditional Christianity).

Mohammed, on the other hand, is firmly within the realm of history. Born about A.D. 570, he began preaching a monotheistic religion privately to a small circle of friends around A.D. 610. Opposition to his teachings by the polytheists (worshipers of many gods) in the area of Arabia where he lived caused him to flee from his home city, Mecca, to neighboring Medina in A.D. 662, an important date in Islamic history. In Medina he gathered a military force and spread his message both by preaching and by military conquest until his death in A.D. 632. His followers continued both his preaching and his military conquests until, at its high point in the Middle Ages, Islam took over much of the old Eastern Roman Empire and threatened Western Europe.

Much of Islamic doctrine resembles Jewish and Christian teachings—one God, angels, an inspired Holy Book, prophets, a Day of Judgment. Critics of Islam would explain this as borrowing by Mohammed from Jewish and Christian sources; defenders of Islam would argue that Mohammed continued and completed a revelation incompletely begun in Judaism and Christianity.

Hinduism—as opposed to Christianity, Islam, and to some extent Buddhism—makes no historical claims and traces back to no single founder. Many of the Hindu holy books are in the form of legends interspersed with dialogues between legendary kings and holy men. As with Buddhism, the doctrines expressed in these holy books are seen as more important than the history or even the existence of the kings and sages who figure in the books. Similar comments could be made about Sikhism and Jainism, and the position of Lao-Tze in Taoism resembles that of Gautama in Buddhism—it is the doctrine, not the historical figure which is important.

A historical study of the Eastern religions is beyond the scope of this book, but in the remainder of this chapter we will consider certain philosophical criticisms of some key points in the Eastern tradition which have been made by Western critics. These will be directed mainly at those points of doctrine we have already discussed, those in which the differences between Eastern and Western approaches to religion are most striking; the point of raising them is not to attack Eastern religion but rather to show the sort of questions about Eastern religion which give pause to the Western mind. A better understanding of these concerns by the adherents of Eastern religions and a better explanation of the Eastern position on these points would be extremely helpful in creating better understanding between East and West. I raise these questions in this spirit, and would be glad to see replies to these points by adherents of Eastern religions.

The criticisms may be grouped into three major categories, which we may call logical, ethical, and metaphysical. An example of logical criticisms of a doctrine of Eastern religion are some recent criticisms of the idea of reincarnation. The doctrine of reincarnation says that some person living now may be some historical figure, say the philosopher Socrates reborn in a new body. (I choose Socrates because his followers have given us such a vivid picture of his personality.) Now suppose I claim to be a reincarnation of Socrates. My body obviously is not the same as that of Socrates—in fact it is not even similar. I have no memories of Socrates' life or times. Thus what would it *mean* to claim that I was a reincarnation of Socrates? Do not doctrines such as reincarnation depend on a native, prescientific idea of the soul as a sort of gaseous "stuff," a sort of semimaterial thing which can be physically transferred from one body to another?

One possible reply is this: Each person has a unique personality, which could survive drastic bodily changes and loss of memory. Thus, to say that I am a reincarnation of Socrates is to say that I have that exact unique personality pattern that was characteristic of Socrates. The critic of reincarnation is not likely to be satisfied with this; he will argue that many people could have personalities quite like that of Socrates without being a reincarnation of Socrates. Even if there were some specified degree of exact similarity, which was of a different kind from mere resemblance, they would argue, we could imagine two persons with that exact degree of similarity and surely both could not be re-incarnations of Socrates!

We will return to some of these questions in more detail when we look, in Chapter 9, at problems concerning life after death; but there is a special problem about the "unique personality pattern" response to the critic's argument if we are talking within the framework of Buddhism or Hinduism. For, according to these religions, the true essential self of every person, the atman in Hindu terminology, is the same! Thus the idea of an essential self, different for each person, seems to conflict with the doctrine of the oneness of all selves. If all selves are really one with Brahman, what does it mean to say that Socrates' soul rather than, say, Plato's has been reincarnated in some present-day person? Are not personality differences mere illusions of the kind that death would dispel?

Thus, the question to, or the challenge to, the defenders of an Eastern religion might be put as follows: "How can you maintain *both* that all souls are one, and *also* that the soul of one specific person can undergo successive reincarnations during which it in some sense remains the same soul, even though it is in different bodies and retaining no memories of previous lives?

Moral difficulties about the doctrine of Karma can be based on mis-understandings. For example, Ed Kelly in our story objected to Eastern indifference to the sufferings of others and blamed this on the doctrine of Karma. But of course if the doctrine of Karma is true, it may be morally appropriate to allow others by suffering to "work out their Karma." Consider the attitude of most people to felons in penitentiaries. Those outside the prison would not want the prisoners to suffer excessively or uselessly, but they would not want to simply release all prisoners either because, by undergoing punishment, it is believed, prisoners not only "pay their debt to society" but also, if they accept their punishment in the right spirit, can be led to reformation and improvement.

Whether or not this is the correct attitude toward prisoners, it is an understandable and widely held view. So, if the beggar or the leper *is* a beggar or leper because of previous wrong actions, it is not unreasonable for the believer in Karma to let him alone to profit from his sufferings.

However, there are ethical difficulties about the idea of Karma which do not seem to be based on misunderstandings. Grant for the sake of argument that someone like Hitler could be born again and that he could, at the time of his death, be held responsible for certain major sins and crimes for which he deserved punishment. Even so, if he is born again into a new body, with no memory of what he has done, is he not in one sense a new person, who morally ought not to be punished for what was done by his former self? If he retained the evil will that made him cause the suffering for which we held him responsible, that would be one thing, but by hypothesis, a reincarnation is supposed to be a fresh start. He has lost his memories and disposition, which were the basis of his evil will. He is "re-formed" in a very literal sense, made into a new person. Is it just to punish this new person Hitler has become, even if the new person *was once* Hitler?

Perhaps so, perhaps not, but at any rate this criticism poses a new problem for the defender of reincarnation. How little of former persons can "carry over" to their reincarnation and still be enough to make the reincarnated person *responsible* for the misdeeds of their former self?

There is also a metaphysical difficulty about the idea of the soul and God in Eastern religion, which we will again put in terms of the Hindu atman and Brahman. Brahman is said to be a nonmaterial reality; matter in fact is mere illusion. But what sense do terms such as "is a part of," "is divided from," is "reunited with" have if we are talking of spirit rather than matter? Matter by definition is that which occupies space and has parts; spirit, at least in the West, has been conceived of as nonspatial and without parts. Thus, for two spirits to be different from each other there must be some difference in their natures, in what makes them what they are; a difference which is essential and not merely superficial. But again, as in the case of reincarnation, we run up against the Hindu and Buddhistic idea of the identity of atman and Brahman. If the soul is essentially the same as God and the same as every other soul, what does it *mean* to say that it is separated from God, temporarily remains separate, eventually is united with God?

The defender of Eastern religion may at this point ask what the difficulty is: That the soul is not *really* separate from God, but only appears to itself to be, is exactly the doctrine he is defending. But this creates its own difficulties; if spirit cannot have parts, then how can it have contradictory properties? A material object can have different properties because it has different parts; my car can be blue and brown, hard and soft, because the body is blue and hard and the seats are brown and soft. But a single simple reality without parts could seemingly not have contradictory properties in this way. In what way then can Atman—the "soul aspect" of Brahman which is the same as each individual atman or true self—have such contradictory properties as for instance, knowing English, not knowing English, being honest, being dishonest, if we cannot say that one *part* of Atman has those properties while another *part* lacks them?

Again, the Eastern religions seem to be thinking of spirit as quasi-material, as in the case of reincarnation. But to do this is to face a host of difficulties. If spirit is a sort of invisible, intangible matter, what is its relation to ordinary matter? Could science ever hope to detect spirit? Is it subject to law which governs ordinary matter? There may be answers to such questions, but the answers are not obvious. So a new question for or challenge to defenders of Eastern religion is the question of just what they mean by spirit, the challenge to clarify their use of this idea. If that is not done, much of what the East says about God and the soul will seem confused or contradictory to the West.

Another difficulty which Westerners have with the Eastern conception of the Supreme Being is the fact that most Eastern religions see the Ultimate Reality as impersonal. This is true of Taoism, it is certainly true of Buddhism, and it is true to a large extent of Hinduism. Brahman is seen as capable of expressing itself as personal; indeed, there are special names in Hindu theology—*Isvara* and sometimes *Purusottama*—for Brahman expressing itself as a Supreme Person. In addition Atman, or the true selfhood of each person thought of as One, is personal in a certain sense. But Brahman itself is thought of as not personal.

The difficulty the Westerner sees in the conception of the Supreme Being as impersonal is that it seems to him that what is impersonal is less perfect than what is personal, and that a Supreme Being which was impersonal would therefore be less than some of the creatures which depended on or proceeded from it. Whatever the full analysis of the idea of a person is, personhood must include at least knowledge and ability to choose. If the Supreme Being has no knowledge and no power of choice, you and I would seem to have something vital that the Supreme Being lacks.

In Western religion God is seen as definitely personal. The Jehovah of the Old Testament and the Allah of Islamic theology definitely have knowledge and will. Traditionally Christianity has an even more daring conception of God in the doctrine of the Trinity. According to this doctrine God is superpersonal in the sense that He has three persons in one divine nature—Father, Son, and Holy Spirit. All have the same divine nature, that is all three have the same knowledge and the same will.

All three are equally God, equally to be worshiped. But the three Persons are genuinely distinct. The traditional way of explaining this is that the distinction between the three Persons is relational—the Son "proceeds" from the Father and the Holy Spirit from both Father and Son; thus each can be described in purely relational terms. The Father is proceeded from but does not proceed, the Son proceeds and is proceeded from, the Holy Spirit proceeds and is not proceeded from.

From a logical point of view this is quite satisfactory: In terms of one relationship each Person has been defined, and it can be seen that exactly three individuals can be defined in this way, no more and no less. But what is meant here by "proceeds"? It does not mean a process that occurs in time; the Father did not exist *before* the Son, nor the Son *before* the Holy Spirit. The relationships are eternal. But what are the relationships? One misunderstanding which sometimes occurs can be easily cleared up: The title "Son" as applied to the Second Person of the Trinity has nothing to do with the fact that this Person took on a human nature or was born as Jesus of Nazareth. The Second Person is the Son eternally, not just since His birth at Bethlehem.

One traditional way of explaining the "proceeding" relationship of Son and Holy Spirit is to associate the proceeding of the Son with knowledge, and that of the Holy Spirit with love. Put somewhat metaphorically, the doctrine is that God's self-knowledge is so complete that it becomes, in effect, not just an image of Himself, but another Person. Between the Father and this Word, or Son, which has proceeded from Him there is a love so total, into which each Person pours so much of Himself, that the love too becomes a Person, the Holy Spirit.

Even Christians disagree about whether we can make sense of this traditional doctrine of the Trinity, but it is at least an attempt to express the idea of God as *more* than personal rather than *less* than personal. At first glance these may seem to be parallel to the doctrine of the Trinity in Hinduism, but Brahma, Vishnu, and Siva—sometimes called the Hindu Trinity—are personifications, not persons. They are merely the activities of Brahman as creating, preserving, and dissolving, given a personal and even anthropomorphic form which is, at least for theoretical Hinduism, purely metaphorical.

A more basic question is whether Brahman itself is intended in Hindu theology to be thought of as superpersonal rather than impersonal. If so, Hinduism, at least, escapes the difficulty of making the Supreme Being subpersonal and so less than its creations. However, this question of whether the Supreme Being is personal, subpersonal, or superpersonal, can form yet another question or challenge to be answered by Eastern religion. Is the Supreme Being a person? If not, is it superpersonal? Then in what sense? If it is subpersonal, is it not less than some of its creations? Of course Hinduism may have one answer to such questions, Buddhism or Taoism another. And at least some recent Christian theology has moved in a direction which leaves it open to the same question (e.g., Paul Tillich's idea of God as the "Ground of Being" rather than as "*a* Being"). But the issue is a profoundly important one for our attitude to the Supreme Being, for if God is not a person, we cannot have a personal relationship with God. And for many religious believers a personal relationship with God is the very essence of religion.

A final difficulty which can be raised by the Westerner approaching Eastern religion is the question of justification. Eastern religion gives us a rather elaborate picture of the cosmos, with all sorts of practical and moral consequences. Why should anyone accept this picture? Some attempted justifications, whatever their merit, do not justify accepting the Eastern doctrines as such. For example, if it is claimed that accepting a religious doctrine always involves a "leap of faith," this does not give a reason for making that leap in the Eastern doctrines rather than some other doctrines. It is also sometimes claimed that all religions have a sort of common core of doctrine and that the universality of this common core is an argument for its truth. But it will be found that to make it plausible that some set of doctrines is the common core of all religion, these doctrines have to be stated so widely and vaguely that they are no longer the doctrines of any specific religion (e.g., "There is Higher Power"; "We should be united with this Higher Power"). Thus, whatever the merits of a "common core" view, it is not an argument for Eastern religion as such.

Some enthusiasts for Eastern religion have claimed that Buddhism and Hinduism themselves represent the common core in all religions, but in view of the contrasts drawn between Eastern and Western religions in the earlier part of this chapter, this seems highly implausible. At least anyone making this claim has a very complicated and difficult task of justification to accomplish.

One could, of course, attempt to give variations of the kinds of arguments we have seen in the first part of this book, aimed at the truth of the doctrines of Eastern religion. The arguments were stated as arguments for the existence of the personal, transcendent God of Western religion; perhaps they could be restated as arguments for the impersonal, immanent God of Eastern religion. It might even be claimed that the arguments as such do not favor one view of God over the other.

But although this is a theoretical possibility which might well be explored, defenders of Eastern religion have shown little tendency to give rational arguments of any kind in support of their beliefs. So this possibility, if it is one, has remained largely unexplored.

Perhaps, though, the Eastern doctrines might be defended on the grounds that they are revealed to us by God, and some variaiton of the argument from miracles might be used to establish that it is a true revelation. Claims are often made by or on behalf of Eastern religious teachers that supernormal powers accompany progress in the understanding and practice of Eastern religion. If such claims could be confirmed, they would seem to offer some evidence for the truth of the doctrines held by those wielding such supernormal powers.

However, when we investigate such claims we find a number of complications. Consider Buddhism, for example. There are a number of miracle stories about Gautama the Buddha, but as we saw, these were first written down five hundred years after the event. Furthermore, there seems to be a sort of contradiction between the idea of miracles and Buddhist doctrine. If matter is pure illusion, and true wisdom is not to desire anything, why would a spiritually enlightened person *want* to work miracles, even if he could? It would be like trying to convince people of the worthlessness of money by giving them money.

In fact we find in one of the earliest codes of conduct for Buddhist monks that among the severe crimes for which they could be excommunicated from their brotherhood were sexual misconduct, dishonesty about money, *and* false claims to supernatural powers! Most scholarly studies of Buddhism have concluded that the miraculous element in Buddhist writings came from the polytheism and popular Hinduism of the cultures in which Buddhism spread, and formed no part of original Buddhism.

Hinduism, as we saw, has an even looser connection with history; stories of gods and miracle-working holy men abound but can hardly be tied down to any historical claims.

Stories of present-day Eastern teachers with supernormal powers would be easier to check, but prove somewhat illusive. While such reports should be given fair hearing and checked out without preconceived prejudices, it does not seem that there are any well-established claims to supernatural powers among present-day Eastern teachers. Such supernormal events always seem to "happen" at some remote time or place, or to someone other than the person who reports them. But if a serious claim is made that the doctrines of Eastern religion are justified by supernormal happenings associated with teachers of those doctrines, it would have to be investigated along the lines laid down in Chapter 4.

To conclude: We have posed a number of questions or challenges for defenders of Eastern religion. Those who already accept some Eastern religion and have no special interest in convincing Westerners to accept it can, of course, ignore these questions and challenges. But any Westerner who is attracted to Eastern religion and any adherents of Eastern religion who hope to convince Westerners of the truth of their beliefs, would do well to ponder these questions and face these challenges.

DISCUSSION QUESTIONS

1. Are you interested in Eastern religions? Why or why not?
2. Do you believe any Eastern religion to be true or partly true? Why or why not?
3. What difficulties, if any, do you find with the doctrine of re-incarnation?
4. What support, if any, do you find for reincarnation?
5. What difficulties, if any, do you find for the doctrine of Karma?
6. What support, if any, do you find for the doctrine of Karma?
7. What are the apparent difficulties in the Eastern idea of spirit?
8. What solution might be found for these difficulties?
9. What arguments can you find for accepting some Eastern religion?
10. What arguments can you find against accepting any Eastern religion?

SUGGESTED READINGS

HICK, JOHN H., *Philosophy of Religion*. 2d ed. Englewood Cliffs, N.J.: Prentice-Hall, Inc., 1973:
Chapter 8, "Human Destiny, Karma and Reincarnation," pp. 107–17.
YANDELL, KEITH E., *God, Man and Religion*. New York: McGraw-Hill Book Company, 1973:
Buddhist Scriptures: "The Four Holy Truths," p. 19.
SMART, NINIAN, "Criteria for Appraisal in Comparative Religion," pp. 147–65.
SMART, NINIAN, "The Nature of Nirvana," pp. 31–37.
The Upanishads: "The Supreme Teaching," pp. 21–27.

8

Mysticism and Drugs:

Ways to Find God?

When Jerry woke up, his first thought was that he was still hallucinating, not yet "down from his trip." The man seated beside his bed, his head bent over a big black book, was oddly dressed, and there was a sound of singing in the background. But from the everyday appearance of everything else, and his own physical sensations, Jerry concluded that this was a real, though somewhat strange, experience. Jerry moved his head and the man stopped reading and bent over Jerry. "I believe you're back with us, brother," he said. "Welcome to the Refuge; I'm Brother Sam."

Jerry tried to make his brain work. The Refuge. He'd heard of it—a sort of religious commune that did what they called "rescue work" among the street people, especially those on drugs. His own voice sounded strange to him when he tried to speak. "Hey, how'd I get here, man?"

The man's answering smile was a little patronizing, Jerry thought. "You were passed out on the street, brother. You won't last very long at this rate. Better put a stop to the drugs before they put a stop to you."

Annoyed, Jerry raised himself on one elbow. "Look, you're the last ones who should be trying to stop me. You're religious people, right? Well, that's why I'm into drugs—I'm looking for God, or what you'd call God."

The other shook his head. "You don't know much about God if you think you can find him by taking drugs."

Jerry hitched himself up a little and lay back on the pillow. He was feeling better and was always ready to argue his beliefs. "That's my way, man. Maybe you have a different way, maybe you fast, or meditate, or say a mantra. But it's the same thing we're trying to get hold of."

Brother Sam shook his head again, slowly and emphatically. "You're wrong, brother. God is a person, not a thing. Sometimes He reveals Himself to His saints, but to those He chooses—not those who go through some set of tricks, or fill their bodies with drugs. You're closer to God lending your brother a helping hand than you'll ever be putting yourself out of your mind with drugs or chants."

Jerry lifted himself up to reply but the sudden motion made him sick and dizzy and he began to retch. The other put his arm around Jerry's shoulders and reached for a basin on the bedside table. Let's talk about it when you're feeling better, brother," he murmured. "Your way of looking for God seems to be pretty hard on you. But at least you're looking."

The points of view represented by Jerry and Brother Sam in our story are ones which are frequently debated when people discuss the religious significance of these special experiences called "mystical experiences." The interchange between Jerry and Sam gives a preliminary idea of two points of view.

According to the first view, there are what might be called "kinds of reality," which we are normally unaware of, but which we can become aware of when we put ourselves into certain states. At least some ways of putting ourselves into these states involve doing things to our bodies: starving them or punishing them in certain ways, or taking certain chemical substances. Other ways of putting ourselves into these states may involve mental operations—for example, repeating certain words over and over. According to this first view, any of these ways is equally good. They all put us into essentially the same state and put us into contact with essentially the same kind of reality. According to this view, there is something, so to speak, "mechanical" or "technological" about this process. You follow certain tested procedures and get certain predictable results. The results are called by different names: a person who gets into this state by taking drugs may call it a drug experience; a person who gets into the state by fasting and repeating prayers may call it a mystical experience. But in this first view these are different names for one experience.

The second view, in contrast with the first view, denies that there is anything mechanical or technological about mystical experience, and denies its similarity with drug experiences. According to the second view, the moral state of the person is usually crucial. Mystical experience is normally both a reward for and a sign of personal holiness. But even more important, mystical experience is not something we can attain by our own efforts; it is something given by God when He chooses and to whom He chooses. No set of procedures can guarantee that you will have a mystical experience, and no set of procedures is a necessary condition for mystical experience. This even overrides the importance of the moral state of the person. God could give a mystical experience to a person who was not morally good in order to convert him to moral goodness, although repeated mystical experience would presumably always be connected with outstanding goodness in the person having these experiences.

Before we can debate these and other issues concernd with experiences of this sort, it would be a good idea to have some idea of what makes an experience mystical, and what the common types of such experiences are. Somewhat surprisingly, one of the best discussions of mystical experiences was given by a poet, W. H. Auden, in the foreword to an anthology of selections from the writings of mystics in the Protestant tradition.* Here is Auden's general description:

> 1.   The experience is "given." That is to say, it cannot be induced or prolonged by an effort of will, though the openness of any individual to receive it is partly determined by his age, his psycho-physical make-up, and his cultural milieu.
> 2.   Whatever the contents of the experience, the subject is absolutely convinced that it is a revelation of reality. When it is over, he does not say, as one says when one awakes from a dream: "Now I am awake and conscious again of the real world." He says, rather: "For a while the veil was lifted and a reality revealed which in my 'normal' state is hidden from me."
> 3.   With whatever the vision is concerned, things, human beings, or God, they are experienced as numinous, clothed in glory, charged with an intense being-thereness.
> 4.   Confronted by the vision, the attention of the subject, in awe, joy, dread, is absolutely absorbed in contemplation and, while the vision lasts, his self, its desires and needs, are completely forgotten.

Auden goes on to distinguish between four kinds of mystical experience, what I will call the Vision of Nature, the Vision of Individual Love,

* W. H. Auden, foreword in *The Protestant Mystics*, edited by Anne Freemantle. Boston, Little Brown Co. 1964. Reprinted by permission of New American Library Inc.

the Vision of Community Love, and the Vision of God. In each of the first three kinds of experiences some things or persons take on a special value or significance. Here, for example, is Auden's description of what I have called the Vision of Nature (his own name is the Vision of Dame Kind, an old poetic name for what we would call Nature):

> The objects of this vision may be inorganic—mountains, rivers, seas—or organic—trees, flowers, beasts—but they are all nonhuman, though human artifacts like buildings may be included. Occasionally human figures are involved, but if so, they are invariably, I believe, strangers to the subject, people working in the fields, passers-by, beggars, or the like, with whom he has no personal relation and of whom, therefore, no personal knowledge. The basic experience is an overwhelming conviction that the objects confronting him have a numinous significance and importance, that the existence of everything he is aware of is holy. And the basic emotion is one of innocent joy, though this joy can include, of course, a reverent dread. In a "normal" state, we value objects either for the immediate aesthetic pleasure they give to our senses—this flower has a pleasant color, this mountain a pleasing shape, but that flower, that mountain are ugly—or for the future satisfaction of our desires which they promise—this fruit will taste delicious, that one horrid. In this vision, such distinctions, between the beautiful and the ugly, the serviceable and the unserviceable, vanish. So long as the vision lasts the self is "noughted," for its attention is completely absorbed in what it contemplates; it makes no judgments and desires nothing, except to continue in communion with what Gerard Manley Hopkins called the inscape of things.

Auden says at one point that this kind of mystical experience is the only one which can be induced by drugs; that may be arguable, as we shall see.

In drug experiences this experience often goes along with changes or distortions in the physical appearance of the objects, but seeing physical objects or seeing things which are there as *physically* different is neither essential to mystical experience nor even especially important to it. Whether or not such hallucinations or distortions occur, you can have the experience Auden describes, and this experience is what is seen as really important. Furthermore, in the other kinds of experience Auden mentions, such changes in physical appearance never, or almost never, occur.

The second kind of experience Auden describes, the Vision of Individual Love, is a feeling of awe and reverence like that in the Vision of Nature, but directed to one individual human being—not just falling in love in the usual sense but a totally absorbing, life-changing experience, like Dante's meeting with Beatrice. The third kind of experience, the Vision of Community Love, is described by Auden in the following passage:

One fine summer night in June 1933 I was sitting on a lawn after dinner with three colleagues, two women and one man. We liked each other well enough but we were certainly not intimate friends, nor had any one of us a sexual interest in another. Incidentally, we had not drunk any alcohol. We were talking casually about everyday matters when, quite suddenly and unexpectedly, something happened. I felt myself invaded by a power which, though I consented to it, was irresistible and certainly not mine. For the first time in my life I knew exactly—because, thanks to the power, I was doing it—what it means to love one's neighbor as oneself. It was also certain, though the conversation continued to be perfectly ordinary, that my three colleagues were having the same experience. (In the case of one of them, I was able later to confirm this.) My personal feelings towards them were unchanged—they were still colleagues, not intimate friends— but I felt their existence as themselves to be of infinite value and rejoiced in it.

Finally, the Vision of God is a feeling of being aware of, in the presence of, in contact with God Himself, experienced as personal, as individual, as distinct either from nature or from other human persons. This experience of God is usually accompanied by feelings of awe or adoration, of delight and of love, like those which Auden described in the other cases.

Such experiences undoubtedly occur, though perhaps not often or to many people. It has been claimed by some that such experiences are both the beginning of religion and the end or purpose at which religion aims or should aim. Others, however, would dispute the importance of such experiences to religion. In criticizing claims of the religious importance of mystical experience they would begin by making two assertions. The first is that each of these four kinds of experiences has been, or at least is claimed to have been, obtained by the use of drugs, contrary to what Auden says. And the second is that in each category named people have also reported negative experiences: a feeling of horror and desolation attached to nature or man-made objects, feelings of terror or hatred attached to individuals or groups, and finally what might be called the vision of the "Spider God," some malignant personal force at the heart of things.

Those who find mystical experience important to religion might reply that while the first kind of experience, the Vision of Nature, is very commonly reported by drug users without any particular theoretical background or any particular axe to grind, it is questionable whether we find spontaneous, uninfluenced reports of any of the others by people who have no knowledge of mystical experiences of the traditional kind, or who aren't trying to prove some sort of point about the unity of drug experience with traditional mysticism. Secondly, they would have doubts as to whether negative mystical experiences have really any claim to be considered as being of the same kind, the same intensity, the same importance as the positive ones.

The critics argue that neither positive nor negative experiences of this kind have any significance for religion in general, though of course they may have great impact on the individual concerned. To say they have no significance for religion in general, means that such experiences cannot be used as a proof for the truth of religious claims and also that they are not the aim or purpose of religion. The claim that such experiences cannot be used as a proof for the truth of religious claims can mean that they can't be a proof for the person himself or herself or that they cannot be a proof for others. The defender of the importance of mystical experience could take a stronger or a weaker stand here. He could agree that mystical experiences, at least in isolation from other factors, cannot be a proof for those who don't have them, but argue that they could be a proof for the person himself. He might cite, for example, St. Paul's experience on the road to Damascus. Previously Paul had believed that Christianity was false and dangerous; after the experience he accepted the truth of Christian claims. It could be argued that theory about mystical experiences should have room for experiences of that sort.

The critic could reply that this experience occurred to a person who already had religious beliefs and was familiar with the Christian claims. The experience on the road to Damascus, you might say, functioned as an additional piece of evidence which changed Paul's view of things he already knew. Just the experience in isolation would not have been enough. The defender might answer that no experience taken in isolation from all other experiences can be said to prove anything beyond itself; any experience has to be tied in with others. The critic's contention, however, is that these experiences are *merly feelings* about persons or things. They cannot be checked in any way and they cannot be evidence for the existence of something beyond themselves. If I take a tumble on the ski slope and *feel* as if my leg is broken, I can check and see if it is. But if while I'm skiing I look at the mountains and snow and trees and so on, and have what Auden calls a Vision of Nature, I have no way of checking or correcting my feelings. If I have a positive experience and feel that trees, for example, are beautiful and awe-inspiring and wonderful, while someone with me has a negative experience of this kind and feels that trees are sinister and evil, how do we decide which of us is right?

Those who defend the religious importance of mystical experiences might argue as follows. Granted, such experiences do occur. (To avoid prejudging any issues, call them "Z-experiences" rather than mystical experiences.) The question, then, is what significance do these Z-experiences, which do in fact occur, have? And that surely has to be decided on the basis of our whole view of the world and the other things we are sure of. Suppose, for example, I have a Z-experience in which my wife seems a sinister and evil person out to harm me. This would contradict a whole mass of experiences I've had of her and I would therefore be inclined to feel that my Z-experience was illusory and misleading. Similarly, if I had a Z-experience in which trees seemed sinister and evil, I would test this against my whole experience and knowledge of the natural world and dismiss this Z-experience as illusory too. Thus, Z-experiences could be checked against other experiences, and sometimes rejected. On the other hand, a Z-experience, can ring true, can fit in with the rest of our experience, can in fact make us see the rest of our experience in a new light. When that happens we can say, "That experience gave me a whole new view of life," even though in one way it was not *just* that experience in isolation, but the new light it shed on all our other experience.

The critic will argue, in reply, first, that experiences of this kind can be drug-induced, and second, that there can be negative Z-experiences. Some people have had drug experiences which were very intense and powerful but very negative—not just ordinary bad trips but really destructive experiences that have made their whole view of life what we would ordinarily call insane or paranoid. But how can we really distinguish this sort of experience as an experience from those like St. Paul's, which transform a life in a positive way? Are we to judge only by results?

The defender can reply that it is not a question of just the results or just the Z-experiences, but of a total experience which includes both. If you just had an abrupt change of behavior, it would be puzzling in a way in which a Z-experience followed by a change of behavior is not. And, equally, if you had a Z-experience which had no effect on subsequent behavior, this would be puzzling.

The critics can cite a variety of possible causes for Z-experiences even when followed by radical changes in behavior—drugs, a psychological crisis, etc.—but the defender need not deny that *some* Z-experiences could have such causes; the question is whether *some* Z-experiences have religious significance. He might grant that *some* may not have any religious significance—may be merely psychological or drug-induced—but argue that for some Z-experiences the best explanation is a genuine intervention in that person's life by God, and that these experiences do have religious significance.

As to whether such experiences are something that the religious believer should aim for or hope for, he might say that they are special gifts given to some very extraordinary people, and that like most gifts of God in this world, they are usually given to us for the sake of others, not for our own sake.

Some religious believers might think of these experiences as valuable in themselves, while others might feel that the experiences as such have no value in themselves, that it is closeness to God which matters. If the experiences bring one closer to God they are good, like anything else which brings one closer to God. If they come to be an end in themselves and stand in the way of closeness to God, they are evil, like whatever keeps one from God.

Among those who defend the place of mystical experience in religious life there are some disagreements which come from differences in religious tradition. In some Catholic writers a rather elaborate theory of "stages of the spiritual life" has been developed. Basically the idea is to give a sort of developmental psychology of the spiritual life. As children grow up they pass through certain stages which are fairly well defined, well enough, at any rate, to make the study of them worthwhile for teachers and others who deal with children. Similarly, it is claimed, the experience of a great many people leading a life of prayer and trying to get closer to God has been sufficiently similar so that we can see some fairly well defined stages in the spiritual life. Those who have to help and advise persons trying to live such a life find it worthwhile to study these stages.

These Catholic writers distinguish three major stages: the Illuminative, Purgative, and Unitive states. A person beginning to go beyond a mere routine everyday good life starts with a stage (Illuminative) where he has pleasant, encouraging experiences, often of a kind we've been calling Z-experiences. After that there is a higher stage (Purgative) where all such experiences stop, and the person has a feeling of abandonment and desolation—the "Dark Night of the Soul." Finally, at the highest stage (Unitive) the person is so closely united with God that he has a constant sense of His presence.

Some of this seems to correspond to experiences many Christians have had, but what many Protestants object to is the idea of a sort of spiritual aristocracy, people who go beyond an ordinary good life to some special status. This objection may mark a genuine difference between Catholic and Protestant spirituality. C. S. Lewis said that the Protestant Reformation had the effect of making greater demands on the average Christian, but abolishing the idea of higher degrees of spirituality. He used a good analogy which, in American terms, would be that what the Reformers did was like raising the standards for a passing grade, but abolishing higher and lower grades and making everything pass-fail.

For other Protestants the real objection is not spiritual elitism, but the idea of going off by oneself and trying to develop one's own relationship to God instead of doing God's work in the world. This is an old Protestant objection to the whole Catholic idea of the contemplative life, the monastic life consisting of prayer, meditation, and so on. Again, it is a very basic difference, and goes back to one's whole view of what God's work in the world is. If only the corporal works of mercy—healing the sick, feeding the hungry, and so on—are God's work, then the monastic life is an evasion of God's work. But if prayer and personal holiness are a contribution to God's work, then a contemplative monastery can be doing God's work as much as a hospital or a soup kitchen.

The Catholic position has something in common with certain Orthodox Jewish ideas. There is a sort of myth or legend in traditional Judaism of the *Zaddakim,* the few just men for whose sake God refrains from destroying the world. And their holiness is seen mainly in terms of prayer and study rather than social activism.

Since we have had no success in deciding whether drugs can give genuine mystical experience by simply comparing the experiences themselves, it may be useful to ask how such practices as prayer and meditation can be expected to bring us closer to God, and then reexamine the question of drug-indeed experiences in this wider context. We will begin with a brief look at the various forms of prayer.

Religious writers who have discussed the question of prayer have sometimes divided prayer into several categories. First is what is technically called petitionary prayer: simply asking God for something, whether that be good weather, forgiveness for sins, or spiritual growth of some kind. Undoubtedly petitionary prayer is the first thing most people think of when the word "prayer" is mentioned, but it is far from the only kind of prayer. Very closely related to the prayer of petition is the expression of thanks to God, either for answers to prayer or for unasked blessings. There is also the expression of guilt or sorrow for sin, which is usually but not necessarily accompanied by petitionary prayers for forgiveness. A third kind is the prayer of adoration: offering oneself to God, surrendering to God, trying to unite oneself completely with God. Some Jewish and Christian theologians have connected the three forms of prayer besides petitionary prayer with the three kinds of offering commanded in the Torah, the early books of the Old Testament: thanks offerings, sin offerings, and *holocausts*—total destruction of a sacrifice to symbolize offering oneself totally to God.

Each sort of prayer has its own problems. Petitionary prayer raises the problem of why such prayers are sometimes unanswered. The answer usually given to this is that just because God is a loving Father does not mean He always grants our prayers, since we often ask for things which would in the long run be bad for us, however much we want them now. In this view, one of the most important points about prayer is that it is not some sort of automatic process, but rather a request to a Person who may have good reasons for refusing a request. A related point can be made about thankfulness on our part for responses to prayer or for other blessings: It cannot just be the enjoyment of what we are given but must be a conscious realization that the blessing comes from God and a deliberate choice to say thank you to Him, rather than simply taking the blessing for granted.

Again, repentance or sorrow for sin must, in this view, be a free and deliberate turning away from sin, which involves, if possible, making up for the wrong we have done, and at least expressing in some inward or outward way our turning away from sin. In Christ's parable of the prodigal son, the prodigal had the intention to express his sorrow in words: "I have sinned against Heaven and you, Father. I am not worthy to be called your son." But he also planned to make an act of humility and sacrifice, to ask his father to treat him merely as a hired servant, no longer as a son. The father's generous forgiveness was such that the son never got to the later part of his planned statement, but the intention was present, even if not carried out.

If we pause here for a moment and look back at the problem of how drug use affects our relationship to God, it would seem that none of the sorts of prayer we have discussed so far would be affected in a positive way by drug use. There would seem to be no special reason why God should grant petitionary prayers more readily because one had ingested some chemical substance. And though in some circumstances the use of a drug might give us *feelings* of thankfulness or sorrow for sin, this would be something the drug did to us, not a free and deliberate act of saying thank you, or turning away from sin. The person who could only be thankful or repentant with chemical aid would be like the person who needed "Dutch courage" from alcohol to act bravely. Most religious believers think that God values our freedom and would prefer whatever thanks or repentance we can achieve on our own to drug-induced thankfulness or repentance.

We can compare drug use with meditation here. Meditation in the sense of thinking about God's goodness to us, or about the badness of our sins, is a technique often recommended to help us be thankful or repentant. Counting our blessings or remembering our sinfulness are familiar aids to thanks or repentance, and may be combined with reflection on important religious events or persons. For example, a Jew could remember God's goodness in delivering the Children of Israel from Egypt, or a Christian could reflect on the life of Christ. But our response to these events would be our own. If drugs merely sharpened our vision it would be one thing, but it seems clear that they also affect our responses.

However, it may be argued, drug use was never intended to enhance petitionary prayer or the prayer of thanksgiving or repentance. It is the prayer of adoration, the effort to unite ourselves to God, which drug use is supposed to enhance. Before we assess this claim, let us look more closely at what is traditionally believed about the prayer of adoration. Most mystics in the Western tradition have seen it chiefly as an offering of ourselves to God. The experiences which mystics have described are seen merely as a sign of the acceptance by God of that offering and as an aid to closer union with God. The Western mystics repeatedly warn that the experiences are nothing, the union with God everything.

Even in the quite different mystical traditions of Buddhism and Hinduism we get a similar result. As we have seen, the Buddhist and Hindu regard the idea of the self as separate from other selves and from God as an illusion, and regard desire as the chief evil. So the desire for any particular kind of experience, including the kind of experiences given by taking drugs, would seem to be evil, and if a drug experience maintains or increases the illusion of selfhood, it hinders the attainment of spiritual liberation.

For the Western mystic the issue of choice will again be vital. If God wishes us to give up our wills to Him, we do not do so by taking a chemical substance which removes our will, any more than a man would fulfill the Christian ideal of chastity by self-castration. The offering must be voluntary and it must be maintained by an act of will, in the Western view; thus the use of drugs could not give us a genuine mystical experience. And if mystical experience is granted by God in response to such voluntary offering or as a spur to it, there seems to be no way in which we could compel God to give us such experiences, certainly not just by taking some chemical into our bodies.

The case is somewhat different with Eastern mysticism, but no more favorable to drug-induced mysticism. If matter, including the matter of which drugs are made and the material body which they affect, is illusory and keeps us from realizing the oneness of atman and Brahman, then it would seem contradictory to the whole basis of Hindu or Buddhist thought that we could attain spiritual liberation through drugs. If drug-taking could achieve spiritual liberation, it would short-circuit the whole notion of Karma, rebirth, etc., which is basic to these Eastern religions.

In conclusion, it is important to see what we have and have not done. We have not shown that drugs cannot induce unusual states of consciousness, nor that some such states of consciousness may not resemble mystical experiences described within Eastern or Western systems of religious belief. What we have tried to show is that judged from within these systems of belief, the kind of experiences which could in principle be induced by drugs would differ in important ways from what are understood to be mystical experiences within the religious tradition.

This suggests the conclusion that Z-experiences, whether mystical experiences in the sense we have just discussed, or drug experiences, cannot be used as arguments for religious belief to the person who does not have a religious belief and who has not himself had genuine mystical experiences—i.e., experiences granted by God in response to a certain free offering of will or to encourage such offering.

This is perhaps not very surprising, and traditionally the existence of mystical experiences has not been offered as an argument for religious belief. In recent years, however, the claim has been made that what we have called Z-experiences are the common core of all religion, and that the existence of Z-experiences is a strong argument for the truth of this common core. But since this claim would be rejected by many religious believers in both the Eastern and Western traditions, it would perhaps be more reasonable for the defenders of this view merely to state their own view of the nature of reality and to show, if they can, how it is supported by the existence of Z-experiences. If, as it appears, the common core view is in effect a new religion, or at least a new interpretation of religion, it would be wise to clearly state the doctrines of this new religion and the evidence which is supposed to support them.

What we can assert with some degree of confidence is that if prayer is thought of in the traditional way as a personal relationship between human persons and God, then no purely chemical or technical means can achieve the ends of prayer, any more than some drug or technique could ensure a truly personal relationship between human persons. If God is thought of in anything like the traditional way, the initiative lies with Him, and He cannot be compelled by any drug or device. On the side of the human person the response must be free and individual, and though it is not impossible that drugs or techniques could aid such a response, we have no evidence that they do; in the nature of the case it is unlikely that they would.

DISCUSSION QUESTIONS

1. Which of the two views of mystical experience described at the beginning of this chapter are you inclined to favor? Why?
2. Have you ever had an experience like those described by Auden? If so, what does this seem to you to prove? If not, do you believe others have had such experiences? Why or why not?
3. If you had a Z-experience, what would this prove to you? Why?
4. If you had a Z-experience, what would it not prove to you? Why?

5. If someone you knew had a Z-experience, what would this prove to *you*? Why?

6. If someone you knew had a Z-experience, what would it *not* prove to *you*? Why?

7. What is the relevance of negative Z-experiences?

8. Would a Z-experience which caused no change in the life of the person who had it have the same value as evidence for religion as one which caused a major change in the life of the person who had it? Why or why not?

9. What other forms of prayer can you think of, besides those described in this chapter? Would you describe any kind of prayer differently than it is described in this chapter?

10. Do you practice any form of prayer? Why or not not?

SUGGESTED READINGS

BRODY, BARUCH A., ed., *Readings in the Philosophy of Religion*. Englewood Cliffs, N.J.: Prentice-Hall, Inc., 1974:

AQUINAS, ST. THOMAS, "The Ceremonial Laws," pp. 535–51.

JAMES, WILLIAM, "Mysticism," pp. 478–503.

SAADYA, "The Types of Commandments," pp. 530–35.

STACE, W. T., "The Teachings of the Mystics," pp. 503–15.

HICK, JOHN H., *Philosophy of Religion*, 2d ed. Englewood Cliffs, N.J.: Prentice-Hall, 1973:

Chapter 2, "The Argument from Special Events and Experiences," p. 29.

YANDELL, KEITH, ed., *God, Man and Religion*. New York: McGraw-Hill Book Company, 1973:

BAILLIE, JOHN, "The Experience of God," pp. 89–96.

BROAD, C. D., "The Argument from Religious Experience, " pp. 27–112.

JAMES, WILLIAM, "The Marks of Mystical Experience," pp. 28–31.

———, "The Validity of Mystical Experience," pp. 71–88.

Life after Death:

Does It Make Sense?

9

The Reverend Robert Butler leaned forward to get a better look at the man on the bed. Yes, his eyelids were fluttering, he was probably going to regain consciousness again. Should he call anyone? No, it was no use waking up the nurse and the doctor had said there was no more he could do for old Sam Butler. If Robert hadn't been Sam's nephew, his only surviving relative, he probably wouldn't be here, since the old man was a fierce un-believer. Robert Butler didn't like deathbeds, though as a minis-ter he had been at many of them. The way some people took death left you feeling better, your own faith strengthened by their genuine faith and hope in the face of death. But too many "pillars of the church" crumbled when they knew that they were dying, their religion showing itself as mere conventionality in the face of death. And there was the occasional repentant sinner who wasn't really, merely a man or woman terrified by death and wanting to cover every possibility, even the God he or she had neglected until now. There were real deathbed conversions, of course, but Butler had seen very few, and the unbelievers who were merely frightened but not really repentant were sad-dening. Better a stiff-necked old heathen like Uncle Samuel.

The dying man's eyes were open now and he spoke in a sort of rasping whisper that Robert Butler had learned to understand in his past few days of visiting the old man. "Well, nephew, not quite gone yet," Sam Butler said. "You have a chance for another try at me. Why aren't you praying or preaching at me?"

Robert Butler smiled at his uncle. "I've been praying all the time, Uncle Sam'l. But I've never found it does much good to preach unless a person is prepared to listen."

The man in the bed coughed a little, but then his voice was a little stronger as he said, "And I'm not, eh Bobby? Right enough, I suppose. When you die you're dead and that being so, I've never had much interest in God or religion. I could help myself in this world and if there's no next world it doesn't matter whether there's a God or not."

Reverend Butler ventered a gentle probe: "Are you so sure that when you die you're dead, Uncle? Why?" The dying man seemed more animated as he gathered breath for a reply. Robert Butler had noticed before that the dying wanted to talk about death, though doctors and relatives would rarely let them. There was even a little grin on Samuel's face as he panted out, "When I was young I saw something . . . in a paper. Thomas Edison said it . . . the electric light fella. Said he tried to weigh or measure a soul in his laboratory . . . couldn't find one."

It was a little late for philosophical argument, thought Robert Butler, but he could try. "Not everything can be weighed or measured, Uncle. The memories you have, your hopes and dreams, they're real enough but you can't weigh or measure them, and if your thoughts aren't the kind of thing that can be weighed or measured, then the mind or soul that has those thoughts can't be either." But the dying man's attention was wandering. "Memories . . . got a lot of those. Remember when you decided to be a minister, Bobby . . . thought you were a fool. But you're a good man . . . an honest man . . . not like some. You can bury me if you want . . . say a prayer over me . . . I won't hear it." As he said the last words his head fell back and gradually, almost imperceptibly, a frozen look came over his face: the look of death. Butler had seen it before: a last flare-up of the candle before it was extinguished, a final word, some last decision made, and then the letting go. Butler didn't need to check pulse or breath to know his uncle was dead. Nothing looks less human than a dead body, he thought. A statue, a picture, looks a thousand times more like the living man than his corpse. His uncle had gone and here were only his remains. Where had he gone? Butler would leave that to the mercy of God. He bowed his head and began to pray.

Any deathbed presents us with the basic problem of life after death. A corpse is not a person; the person we could relate to a moment before the death is no longer there. Is that person simply destroyed, stopped, extinguished? Or does that person still function, still know and act, on some level or in some place not accessible to our senses? These are the real choices, though there is a sickly kind of paganism encouraged by some funeral directors which treats the corpse as if it were still the person, as if it could feel silken cushions or be disturbed by damp or cold. But either the corpse is *all* that is left of the person, or it is simply what has been left while the nonbodily part of the person goes on.

Recently another possibility has been discussed by some contemporary Christian theologians. They grant that the person is destroyed or extinguished at death; they deny that any nonmaterial part of the person survives, because they have been convinced by some arguments against this idea, which we will examine shortly. They pin their hopes for life after death, then, on the idea of resurrection only, the idea that although between death and some final day of resurrection no trace of the dead person is in existence, nevertheless that person will be re-created in bodily form.

There are both philosophical and theological difficulties with this view. The philosophical difficulties have to do with the question of whether even if such a re-creation occurred, the resurrected person would be the same person who had died. The theological difficulties have to do with the fact, which seems clear to most unbiased observers, that this view is not the traditional Judeo-Christian view. Since few philosophers or theologians today would put a great deal of weight on purely philosophical arguments for life after death, those who believe in life after death generally base their confidence on religious revelation: a message from God transmitted through a Church or Scripture.

But if this is the source of our confidence in life after death, we cannot simply change the message to suit our own ideas; and at least within traditional Judaism and Christianity the hope of resurrection has always been accompanied by the idea that some nonmaterial part of the person, a soul or spirit, continues to exist between death and resurrection. This view also would seem to avoid the philosophical problem that arises about the identity of the resurrected body.

But even setting aside this current dispute among theologians, we can see that since the recorded beginnings of religion and of philosophy there has been a belief in the survival of some nonmaterial component of a human person after the dissolution of his body. A rejection of such beliefs on philosophical or scientific grounds has had almost as long a history. But in the past few decades a good many able philosophers have become convinced that there are new and decisive objections to this notion of disembodied survival, objections which show the concept of disembodied survival to be unintelligible. But since there are various, somewhat incompatible, versions of the belief in disembodied survival which cannot all be simultaneously defended, I will take it that what is being defended here is the traditional Judeo-Christian view that man consists of body and soul, that death is the separation of the two, and that the soul will be reunited with a body (which can reasonably be called the same body from which it was separated). This view is not, of course, held in isolation but is part of a complex of beliefs (God, the Last Judgment, Heaven or Hell, etc.) which help give meaning to the belief in disembodied survival. This is important, for a good deal of what is said by critics of disembodied survival has very little to do with this complex of beliefs and may even presuppose a competitive picture.

A discussion of death and immortality is intended to illuminate religious belief. But it is striking how fundamentally nonreligious, in the traditional sense of religious, many discussions of these points are. There is practically no mention of God, of any relation of the disembodied soul to God, or even of the role of God or Christ in the discussion of an afterlife. But a mere belief in some sort of survival after death, without relation to God, is of no special religious significance, as religion is traditionally understood. It is perhaps not surprising that a fundamentally childish and religiously trivial idea of immortality which puts most emphasis on seeing loved ones again should fall easy victim to sophisticated philosophical criticism. But that has little bearing on the larger question of whether the much more complex and sophisticated idea of immortality embedded in traditional Judeo-Christian belief can survive such criticism.

In the traditional view there are some activities for which a body is logically necessary—for example, laughing. These will cease at death but perhaps begin again after resurrection. There are some activities for which a body does not seem to be necessary—for example, understanding a joke. These may well go on after death and before resurrection. There are some activities for which a body *may* be necessary—for example, a feeling of hilarity. These may or may not go on after death and resurrection, depending on whether having a body is a necessary condition for them.

In light of this we can see the flaw in the assumption that anyone who holds the traditional view must hold the extreme view (held by Plato and other ancient philosophers) that the body is not essential to what we mean by persons, that it can be thought of as the prison within which the soul is temporarily restricted, the house within which it is temporarily lodged, or as the suit of clothes which adorns a person for the moment, and that the essence of a person is identifiable with the mind or soul. This is not the traditional Judeo-Christian view. According to that view a human person is essentially soul and body. When they separate, the body is not in any sense a person. It is, as undertakers used to say in a franker day, "the remains." The soul is still a person but a damaged, mutilated person, lacking many things proper to a human person. A deaf, blind multiple amputee is certainly still a person, though a terribly damaged one. A disembodied soul is still a person, but even more terribly damaged. Socrates would have gayly declined resurrection; he held a view like Plato's. But for the Christian and for many Jews also, hope is vain unless the dead rise again.

One objection to the idea of disembodied survival is the objection that all of our learning of concepts and use of concepts depend on our being in a social context with other human beings, and this context involves seeing, hearing, etc., things which would be impossible to a disembodied soul. Thus, it is argued, the very idea of a disembodied person's carrying on mental activities is nonsensical, for such a person could not learn or use concepts.

But the proponent of the traditional view need not hold that a disembodied spirit could learn any new concepts, nor need he hold that the disembodied soul is permanently barred from using his concepts in a common social context. In the traditional view the disembodied soul is an exaggerated form of the predicament of the man who is paralyzed and stricken blind and deaf for a time, or that unfortunate girl who was imprisoned by her kidnappers in a sort of underground coffin. The disembodied person has moved and will move again in a common social context. Even if a disembodied spirit could not learn the meaning of the concept of lying, this does not mean that it could not remember the lies it told while embodied and repent them. Even if repentance makes no sense without the possibility of verbal expression of repentance, begging forgiveness from the injured party, etc., the disembodied soul might plan to engage in these activities after its resurrection, just as the kidnapped girl planned an elaborate meal to eat when and if rescued. Not that we need necessarily grant these points, but the believer in disembodied survival need not, on account of his belief, deny them. So far as I can see, it is compatible with the strictest traditional orthodoxy that disembodied souls have no awareness of other souls; reunions might have to wait for the General Resurrection. Thus, against the traditional view of death as the separation of the soul and body, as disembodied existence of the soul for a time and then resurrection of the body, this first objection seems wholly ineffective.

Another objection made by those who challenge the intelligibility of disembodied survival could be put in these words:

> Our language—and this of course applies just as much to person-words and all the other words we use in our discourse about persons as to the words for material things—has been evolved as an instrument for dealing with the situations of this world in which men have found themselves. When we try—as we are trying when we want to speak of people surviving death— to use it for dealing with radically different conditions, it breaks down.

But, we may argue, the fact that discourse of a certain sort developed in one set of circumstances does not mean that such discourse could not be used in different circumstances. Consider, for example, the obviously bad argument, "All of our language has been evolved for use in the situations in which men have found themselves: for situations on this planet. Therefore, if we try to use this language in the radically different circumstances of space travel, it breaks down. So astronauts will be unable to communicate meaningfully with Earth." The critic would, of course, object that there is a different *kind* of radical difference involved in disembodied survival. But if he grants that private experiences might exist in a disembodied state, he grants that the experiences of a disembodied soul might have something in common with those we have learned to talk about meaningfully. Thus, since there is not a *total* difference, he owes us an account of just what degree of radical difference causes language to break down, or if it is not a matter of degree, what kind of radical difference. It is to be doubted whether such an account could be given in non-question-begging terms, and therefore the apparent generality of the critics' remarks about language reduces to the unsupported assertion that our language breaks down if we try to talk of disembodied existence. This would, of course, be denied by many, and the critic would need a powerful argument to support his assertion, which he does not have.

So far we have been talking as if a disembodied person could be straightforwardly identified as the soul of someone who had died. But it is this very point that some modern critics deny. We cannot, of course, identify disembodied spirits as certain persons by bodily continuity—by tracing their present body back through earlier stages to the person who died—for of course they have no body. But, these critics argue, other criteria of personal identity—other ways of telling persons apart— all *depend* on bodily continuity. If two people both claim to remember being a certain person—for example, the first person to enter a new football stadium as a paying member of the audience—we can trace back the history of each person and find out which of either of them was the person in question. But suppose two disembodied spirits both claimed to have witnessed, done, or suffered certain things, and only one of them could be right. At least one would have false memories, but we could certainly not check this by tracing back the histories of their bodies. These critics generalize such cases to a claim that we would have no criterion or standard of identity for disembodied persons. Are they right?

Consider the case of a disembodied spirit with alleged memories of the life of a dead person. The mere fact that the spirit does not *now* have a body surely does not prove that it could not, while embodied, have witnessed, done, or suffered certain things. Suppose that Jungle Jim kills a tiger with his left hand, but the hand is badly mauled and must be amputated. The fact that Jim does not now have the hand that killed the tiger does not mean that he is not the same person who killed the tiger. If Jim dies, why should not his soul remember killing the tiger, even if it no longer has the body which killed the tiger? Such a memory would be subject to the test of bodily identity only in the usual, negative way. Jim might be told (by some Higher Authority perhaps) that he had only dreamed that he killed the tiger; it was in fact killed by his gunbearer while Jim was already on his way to the hospital.

Of course it might be argued that since false memories are possible, the disembodied spirit's memories of being Jungle Jim may be all false: It is not the soul of that dead man at all. But two comments can be made about this. First, it seems no different from cases which might occur of an embodied person having false memories. The criterion of bodily continuity could decide the question of whether these were really memories in a negative way: It could prove, for example, that the person's body was never at the places he remembered being. But it could not prove that any set of memories were true memories, only that they *could* be. In other words, bodily continuity plus sincere assertion of memory claims is not sufficient to establish that these memory claims are true.

To say that *present* possession of the body which witnessed, did, or suffered certain actions is a *necessary* condition of having memories of those events seems to me to beg the question. Similarly, the fact that bodily continuity is now taken to be a sufficient condition of personal identity does not mean that it is a necessary condition for personal identity after death, and to assume that it is also begs the question.

However, this in itself does not answer the critics' claim that there is no criterion or standard of personal identity which does not depend on bodily continuity. To do this we will have to suggest at least one such standard; in fact, we will consider two possibilities.

The two criteria with which we will be concerned we will call the "personality pattern" criterion and the "body animation capacity" criterion. It might be argued that a disembodied spirit could be identified as the soul of a dead man, either because each person has a unique personality pattern which persists after death, or because a disembodied spirit retains a capacity for animating a certain body even after the death of that body. Each suggestion has its own difficulties, but let us first consider a difficulty common to both.

The contention common to both criteria is that we never in fact use either criterion as a means of re-identifying individuals. With regard to unique personality pattern, I will argue that this is simply false. With regard to capacity for body animation, I would reply that it is of course true in the nature of the cases that we do not *now* use it as a criterion of personal identity. But how could we establish the truth of the principle, "No criterion which is not *now* used as a criterion of personal identity could be used as a criteron of post-mortem identity"? It does not seem to me to be self-evident, and I know of no argument for it.

A difficulty unique to the "unique personality pattern" criterion is the denial of the truth or meaningfulness of the idea that each individual has a unique personality pattern. I have no space here to deal with the truth of this idea. It seems to me to be extremely plausible on the basis of experiences common to every human being who has had close personal relations with another human being.

It might be objected that the idea of a personality pattern presupposes the idea of a body by which the personality pattern in question is expressed. But this seems to be mistaken. We might try to reduce the notion of a personality purely to a series of actions, with nothing existing over and above those actions, but this will not work. Even if the only way we could become aware of a personality pattern is by observing what it does, it seems to be simply false that only bodily actions could show a personality pattern. If one disembodied spirit could be telepathically aware of another's thoughts, it might quite easily gain a knowledge of the personality pattern of that other disembodied spirit.

An interesting suggestion as to what might constitute the uniqueness of the individual soul is the view held by some believers in disembodied survival that each individual is created to appreciate, enjoy, and communicate to others some aspect of the Divine Nature which he alone can see. This gives each individual a unique perspective on the world which accounts for the individuality that we grasp in people we know and love. A disembodied spirit with this perspective is necessarily the soul of the dead man who had that perspective. I say necessarily, because to duplicate persons with this perspective would be in this view a positively irrational action, which could never be willed by God, and thus could never occur.

Similar considerations apply, by the way, to the body animation capacity criteria. Those who raise the difficulty about possible duplication of spirits with the power to animate a given body are either imagining the duplicate as springing into existence out of nothing of its own accord, or they are imagining it as created by a being with the power to create such a duplicate. Presumably most believers would reject the first possibility as unthinkable and reject he second for reasons like those just cited against duplication of unique personalities.

Those who object to the second criterion would still, I think, object that they are not being told *what* it is that has this body-animating capacity. To say that something can be identified as "the being which has capacity C" does in fact seem to raise difficulties. We tend to use material objects as a paradigm, and with them "What is it?" seems separable from "What can it do?"

But the believer in disembodied survival can point to the basic experience of each human being. We are aware of ourselves as knowing and willing; our own knowings and willings we are directly aware of, but no one else's. We are also aware of ourselves as trying to move our bodies and succeeding. But we are unable to succeed in moving anyone else's body simply by trying. Thus it might be claimed that soul as that which animates body is a matter of direct experience. Of course we may misinterpret this experience, but if we do, it is a very ancient and widespread misinterpretation.

It might be objected that one can make no sense of the idea of being the bearer of certain capacities without the possibility of exercising them. But consider a totally paralyzed man who believes he will be cured. He remembers moving his limbs; he looks forward to moving them again. Meanwhile he thinks, remembers, worries, regrets. The disembodied soul in the view we are considering remembers having a body and knows he will have one again. Meanwhile he remembers, and repents, or rebels.

A final difficulty specific to the body animation capacity criterion is the question of the *re*-animation of a body. In what sense would a resurrected body be the *same* body as the one which died? Here it seems to me plausible to turn to the idea, held by some believers in disembodied survival, of the body as an expression of or correlate to the soul. Socrates without his snub nose, Aquinas without his girth are not fully Socrates and Aquinas. Thus, at a minimum, the resurrected body would be like the pre-death body in essential ways: It would be recognizable to the dead man's friends, for example. But it might also be an even better vehicle for the person's unique individuality, "his" body, because after a period of time the soul once again is able to express itself through a material body uniquely correlated to it.

Though these two criteria are not the ones we use now, it is plainly reasonable to identify as me a future disembodied person with memories identical with mine, with my unique personality pattern, and with the capacity to re-animate a body recognizably mine, which began to be conscious at the very instant of my death. While it might be logically possible that this individual is not me, it would be irrational to hold that it is not me.

Here the critic may be hoist with his own petard. For if he suggests that this individual might not be me, I will ask what he *means* by saying the individual is not me. If he offers any mark by which this disembodied person could be distinguished from me, we can build the absence of this mark into our criteria. But the mark of difference cannot be that I have a body and the disembodied spirit does not, for that begs the question.

It has sometimes been suggested that the existence of two spirits with all these characteristics would show that neither was the same as me, and that such duplication is logically possible. But mere logical possibility proves nothing. It is logically possible that I split like an amoeba last night and that therefore neither "I" nor my "twin" can be identified with me as I was yesterday, though both of us are continuous with my previous body. Of course such a physical split could be observed with the senses and such a psychic split might be known only to God. But if we demand that any question regarding disembodied spirits be answerable in principle by observation with the senses, we have already made it impossible to give any nonbodily criteria for identity.

And this, I think, is in the upshot what the "disembodied survival is unintelligible" argument amounts to. As in many skeptical arguments, an impossible demand is made and then the opponent is faulted for not satisfying the demand. Any real criterion for identity in disembodied spirits will be accepted, but unfortunately only bodily continuity is acceptable as a real criterion.

In light of these replies, it does not seem that the modern attack on the intelligibility of disembodied survival is successful, and we have no reason on account of these criticisms to reject the traditional Judeo-Christian picture of death followed by disembodied survival followed in turn by the reuniting of the soul with a body which is a renewal or resurrection of its former body. What about more traditional objections?

Most older objections to the idea of disembodied survival depend in some way on the view that everything real is material, that any kind of nonmaterial reality can simply be denied because it is not accessible to our senses. In one way, such materialism seems to be ingrained in many aspects of Western thinking. It is worth remembering, though, at least for the sake of balance, that the unreality of matter and the idea that everything real is spiritual have seemed equally obvious to many persons, especially in the East.

In fact, our experience *seems* to be dualistic. We are aware of an inner world of thought and feeling, and an outer world of matter and material objects. Should we deny the inner experience and say, as materialists do, that only the outer world of matter is real? Should we deny the outer world of matter and say that only the inner, nonmaterial world of thought and mind exists? Or should we grant the dualistic nature of reality and admit two realities, matter and spirit, which interact in subtle and complex ways? To many people the last alternative seems common sense; the two extreme views seem to them to ignore too much in our experience.

But the point is not just the existence of spirit, but whether *our* spirits survive *our* bodies. What can philosophy say here? There are traditional arguments which try to show that since our thoughts are not material, neither are our minds—Reverend Butler in our story began to give such an argument. And there are traditional arguments that, since a spirit has no parts to be taken apart, a spirit could go out of existence only by being annihilated; this would seem to go against our experience of the universe, where nothing simply vanishes any more than anything simply pops into existence. But even to more traditional philosophers such arguments have never seemed as strong as those for the existence of God.

So most religious believers base their belief in life after death on revelation (perhaps, as we saw in Chapter 5, on revelation backed up or authenticated by miracles), or else on general arguments from the justice or mercy of God. Many people die having had more sorrow than happiness for no fault of their own: Would a good God permit this apparent injustice? And would a loving and generous God create persons simply to annihilate them? Thus, in the view of many religious believers, survival after death can only be based on a living belief in God. If God is good, they argue, there is an afterlife, and they would not shrink from the consequence: that if there is no afterlife, then God is not good. Some religious believers today try to combine a denial of afterlife with an affirmation of God's goodness, but it seems to many believers, as well as to many unbelievers, that this cannot really be done. If even one person suffers unjustly and is then destroyed, annihilated forever, then God cannot be good in any sense of goodness which is even analogous to human goodness.

Many people might grant that traditional ideas of life after death can be defended from philosophical attacks, and that a real belief in God's goodness leads to a belief in a life after death. But there is still a sort of emptiness to this admission, for they do not know *what* they are believing in. The traditional imagery of harps and choirs, pearly gates and golden streets is too hackneyed, too often misused or laughed at to carry any emotional weight. And they have no image and no theory to put in its place. Even if they knew or understood the traditional theology of the afterlife, it too is put in strange and perhaps outmoded ways, and might mean little to them.

Therefore, the last chapter of this book will consist of some speculations about life after death, attempting to make the idea meaningful to modern readers. I close on this note of speculation for several reasons. First, I agree with the philosopher Plato that where we do not have certainty or where we are sure only of an abstract principle, it can be useful to tell a "myth" or "likely story" embodying what might be, and probably even is, the truth, in a concrete form.

Second, I hope to stimulate thinking by arousing controversy. If my speculations seem wrong-headed or unfounded to readers, perhaps they will be encouraged to put forward their own ideas or speculations. At least one way to get closer to the truth is to speculate and then to test our speculations by criticism and argument.

Finally, I am convinced that a good deal of the opposition to the idea of an afterlife among ordinary persons, as opposed to professional philosophers or theologians, is simply an opposition to outmoded or inadequate symbols of the afterlife, just as much of the polemic against God seems to be directed at the notion of an old man with a gray beard sitting on a cloud in the sky. Even if this is an area where we can only guess or think only in symbols, an area where all of our ideas are inadequate, still some symbols and ideas are more inadequate than others. New images or ideas may stimulate new insights; at least they will stimulate newer arguments.

DISCUSSION QUESTIONS

1. Do you believe that the human person survives death? Why or why not?

2. What ideas (e.g., resurrection, disembodied survival) about life after death (if any) do you accept? Why?

3. What ideas about life after death do you reject? Why?

4. Could thinking go on without a body? Why or why not?

5. Is our language about persons necessarily used only of embodied persons? Why or why not?

6. Are there problems about duplication of the same soul or spirit

which could not arise in the case of duplication of bodies? Why or why not?

7.   Are there reasonable standards or criteria of identity for disembodied persons? Why or why not?

8.   Is everything real material? Why or why not?

9.   Is everything real spiritual? Why or why not?

10.   Do you have any picture of or theory about life after death? Explain and defend it.

SUGGESTED READINGS

BRODY, BARUCH A., ed., *Readings in the Philosophy of Religion.* Englewood Cliffs, N.J.: Prentice-Hall, Inc., 1974:

> FLEW, ANTONY, "Locke and the Problem of Personal Identity," pp. 624–39.
>
> GEACH, PETER, "Immortality," pp. 655–63.
>
> QUINTON, ANTHONY, "The Soul," pp. 640–54.

HICK, JOHN H., *Philosophy of Religion,* 2d ed. Englewood Cliffs, N.J.: Prentice-Hall, Inc., 1973:

> Chapter 7, "Human Destiny: Immortality and Resurrection," pp. 97–106.

YANDELL, KEITH, ed., *God, Man and Religion.* New York: McGraw-Hill Book Company, 1973:

> PATON, H. J., "Intellectual Impediments to Religious Belief," pp. 167–75.

10

Life after Death:

What Would It Be Like?

Nothing like a funeral for getting the relatives together, thought Jean Dale, glancing around the crowded, noisy living room of the little house. By this time, a few hours after the funeral, people were relaxing and the scene was a cheerful one in a muted sort of way. But the crowd and the noise were enough to bring on one of Jean's headaches, and feeling in the pocket of her seldom-worn best suit, she made sure her pills were there, then headed to the kitchen for a glass of water. She had actually gotten the water and taken her pills before she noticed the quiet figure at the kitchen table. It was Freda McWhortle, the widow of the man they had just buried, and for a moment Jean had a cowardly impulse to slip out of the kitchen, pretending she hadn't noticed Freda. But her Methodist conscience told her that she ought to say a word of comfort if she could. She went over to Freda. "Freda, I'm awfully sorry about Fred," she began. "We had our disagreements, but he was a good man."

Freda McWhortle looked up from the cold cup of coffee she had been staring at, thankful for Jean's quiet, matter-of-fact tones. Some of the McWhortle relatives were inclined to drama-tize things, and she had been hugged and wept over more than she liked. Her voice, when she answered Jean, showed the strain she was under. "He was a good husband and father and he always made a good living for us. Most people liked Fred, even if they argued with him. He was a great one for arguing, Fred was." Her face crumpled a little as she went on unsteadily, "It seems strange that I won't hear him roaring around about something any more—that I won't ever see him again."

Jean sat down beside Freda and put her hand over the hand of the older woman. "Freda, you're a good Christian woman. You know you'll see Fred again, in heaven."

Mrs. McWhortle shook her head uncertainly. "I don't know, Jean. All that about harps and crowns that you hear in church doesn't seem to mean much to me. I can't picture Fred in the kind of heaven they talk about."

Jean leaned forward earnestly; perhaps here was a way she could help a little. "Freda, all that about harps and crowns and golden streets—those are just symbols. Those old Jewish writers were trying to tell us how wonderful and splendid heaven was by using images that meant something to them. We don't have to use their images if they don't mean anything to us. When I try to imagine heaven I think of green pastures, like in the Psalm, and trees and flowers—but the images don't matter, it's the real thing behind them that's important."

Freda nodded. "I know that's true, Jean, but it's the real thing that I can't get hold of. I sometimes wonder if heaven isn't just being remembered by the ones we love."

Jean shook her head gently. "That might be the best we could come up with if we didn't believe in God, Freda. But if we do believe in a good, loving God, we can't believe that He would forget about Fred or let him just not exist any more. God doesn't waste anything or throw anything away—certainly not people. Remember, God loves Fred even more than you do, Freda, and wouldn't want Fred to stop existing, or stop being Fred."

Freda McWhortle looked at Jean with renewed respect. "You're a smart woman, Jean Dale. I never thought of it that way but I'm sure you're right. But I still can't imagine what it's like for Fred—Jean, is it so different he won't ever remember me?"

Jean smiled, feeling she *had* helped Freda at least a little. "He's with God, Freda, that's all we can really say. And good things will come to him because he's a good man. And he won't forget you, Freda, any more than you'd forget him, no matter how different things were."

Freda smiled back a little tremulously. "Thank you, Jean,

for helping me get straight in my mind about things. If Fred is still Fred and still remembers me, I guess that's the important thing. The Lord's always been good to us so far, and I guess He hasn't changed. Well, let's go back to the living room, Jean. I probably won't see some of those cousins again until somebody else in the family dies."

Disbelief is sometimes almost more a matter of the imagination than of the intellect. If we cannot in any way visualize or make real to ourselves a state of affairs, we find it hard to believe in. This is just as true of an atomic war or a tremendously overpopulated world as it is of an afterlife—many people do not take these possibilities seriously because they cannot imagine them.

Probably one major barrier to belief in a life after death for many people is an inability to make real to themselves what life after death would be like. The symbols and imaginative pictures that worked for earlier generations no longer work for them, but they have nothing to put in their place. In such a situation, speculating, trying out various possibilities, using our imaginations can remove barriers which are more psychological than intellectual. Therefore, this chapter is not an argument for life after death—as we have said earlier the strongest claims for life after death are based on arguments for the existence of God and from the justice and goodness of God. Nor is it, like the previous chapter, a deference of traditional ideas of life after death in the face of criticism. Rather, this chapter consists of speculations about what life after death might mean.

In what follows I want to speculate about how our perception of time and the operation of our memory in the life after death might be be different from anything we can experience now except in a very incomplete and fragmentary way. I will call this an "eternal life view" of immortality, for reasons which will become apparent. These speculations are suggested to me by certain philosophical considerations and by certain scriptural passages, but I do not want to put them forward as something which can be established either by philosophical argument or by scriptural exegesis. On the other hand, I am not just indulging an unbridled imagination; I think that on both philosophical and theological grounds the ideas I will put forward have a certain amount of plausibility.

Speculation about the afterlife can, of course, be dangerous. It can divert our attention from the problems of the moment and make us neglect doing our duty, minute by minute. But if we take seriously the traditional religious idea that our life in this world is a preparation for eternal life with God, then it would be very strange to spend no thought at all on the goal we are preparing for. I think that perhaps religious believers have overreacted to taunts about "pie in the sky" and religion as the "opiate of the people" which express the view that religion is a device to avoid social justice and keep the poor in their place.

Some religious believers seem so determined to disprove this view of religion that they ignore or even reject the idea of a life after death and concentrate on outdoing the secularist at alleviating suffering and fighting injustice. Both of these are excellent things, but experience shows that if pursued as ends in themselves they often lead to disillusionment or despair. There is always so much misery we cannot alleviate, so many injustices we cannot overcome. In the face of the immensity of the task we tend to give up unless we are sustained by some vision or hope. And if the religious believers' hope is different from that of the secularist, they would do well to see what is distinctive about it and what bearing it has on action here and now.

One significant difference between the secularist vision of a perfected human society and the religious believers' hope is the importance of the individual. Take for instance a young Indian mother who is starving to death, along with her child, after a life of hunger, hardship, and degradation. What is it to her that a classless society, or a psychologically adjusted society, or any perfect society you like, may someday exist? She would trade all such grandiose hopes for a little food or for some immediate hope for her child. The secularist can hope and work for a society in which no one is starved or degraded, and this is a noble objective. But it offers no personal hope to those starving or degraded now or in the past.

Religious belief, on the other hand, has traditionally offered an individual hope to each person: Death is not the end, and the sufferings of this time are not to be compared to the glory and happiness which awaits us. But this hope and consolation is frequently presented in too abstract and general a form, and the poetic images which helped other ages to appreciate this hope seem no longer to work for modern man. Part of our need, no doubt, is for great poets and artists who will reinterpret the vision for our age. But philosophy too can help us to understand and appreciate the hope presented to the world by religious belief. This is what we will try to do in this chapter.

Let us begin, then, with our present situation. We live, you might say, in the present. The past is gone, and memory retains only a dim and faded remnant of it. Much is forgotten; what is remembered has not the immediacy of present experience. Even the present is hard to grasp; when we try to concentrate on an experience our own concentration can get in the way of the experience. Enjoyable experiences seem to be over almost before they begin, while unpleasant experiences seem to drag on forever. We have the feeling of being at the mercy of time; we cannot, however we try, stop the process of change or keep our relation to things as we want it to be.

Still, we are not entirely under subjection to time. A long time by the clock can seem short to us, or a short time by the clock seem long. We sometimes have the feeling of grasping an experience as a whole, the earlier parts of it so keenly remembered that they still seem present in the later parts. We do not experience the present only as a point-like instant; we have a "specious present," an interval of time which somehow seems all to be present at once. To some extent the interval composing the specious present seems to expand and contract. Just as an experienced reader reads in groups of words, not letter by letter, but is aware of the special relations of the letters, we seem to grasp experience not instant by instant but in intervals, yet without being unaware of temporal relationships within those intervals. (One might even speculate that time seems to go faster for us as we grow older because we take it in larger bites than a child does, just as a fast reader reads in larger groups than a slow reader.)

Contrast our situation with that of God as pictured in traditional theological and philosophical terms. In this view, God is outside of time, not subject to time. This means that He is not contained within any stretch of time, no matter how long—He is "from everlasting to everlasting." But it also means that He has not temporal parts—His life is not chopped into temporal chunks as ours are; He is *totally* present at each moment of time. Or to put it in another way, all time is present to Him in something like the way the specious present is present to us. The most difficult and puzzling part of this traditional picture is God's relation to the future. But luckily, that part of God's relation to time need not concern us in the present context. Let us concentrate on God's relation to past and present.

If the traditional view is right, God is not *remembering* the past, He is *seeing* it. The past is still present to God, as the events of a split second ago are still present to us in our specious present. God is aware of the temporal relations of events to each other, but they do not have those temporal relations to *Him.* Used with due caution, a dimensional analogy is perhaps illuminating here. Consider any line of letters on this page. Each letter is to the left or right of others. But your eyes are not (at least in any simple fashion) to the left or right of a given letter; your eyes are *above* that letter, in another dimension entirely. If a letter had a sort of one-dimensional vision, it could see only the letters near it, whereas we can see the whole group of letters, and their relations, at one glance. God's nontemporal knowledge of temporal events is no doubt incomprehensible to us in the sense that we cannot *completely* understand it, but we can have some grasp of it by analogy from our own experience.

With this foundation we will make our first speculative suggestion about our perception of time and the operation of our memory in the afterlife. The suggestion is that our relation to time might be more like God's relation to time than it is at present, and that rather than remembering our past in the way we now remember, we might experience or see it in God, by somehow participating in God's "eternal now" where past events are still present. Furthermore, we might have some control over which parts of our past we thus see or experience, and in how much detail we see or experience them. To give another analogy, our present experience of time is like seeing lines of writing roll by on a movie screen: We cannot stop or slow up or speed up the rolling lines. If we try to remember earlier lines, it is hard to do so without neglecting the lines now rolling past. Many fast readers find this kind of rolling print extremely annoying, because it goes at average or below average reading speed, and they have to wait for the next line. Similarly we often find the pace of life annoying: too fast at one time, too slow at another.

However, our access to our past in the afterlife might be like our access to words in a printed book where we can read at our own pace, stop reading ahead and go back and reread an earlier passage, glance from an earlier passage to a later one, and so on. Or, to vary the analogy, like our relation to a complex picture (one of Bruegel's, for instance) which we can stand back and view as a whole, or examine in detail. The second analogy is superior to the first in this respect: In the case of a book we never normally have any sense of the book as a whole except through the operation of memory, whereas in the case of the picture we can imagine ourselves drawing back to view it as a whole, stepping forward to look at a detail, stepping back again, and so on. Even while examining a detail, we can, so to speak, out of the corners of our eyes have a sense of the picture as a whole. So with our perception of our earthly life after we are dead—we might be able to grasp it as a whole but also see it in detail. However, in seeing it in detail we need not lose our sense of it as a whole. Furthermore, we might be able to see one detail for as long as we like, and skip over dull stretches. (Hereafter I will refer to this process as "reading" our lives.)

This last implies two time scales; we could use as much "afterlife time" as we like to examine a short period of "pre-mortem-life time." But even if this were so, we must not jump to the conclusion that afterlife time will be the same *sort* of time as pre-mortem-life time. If you are reading a book or viewing a picture, you can pause on a line or a detail as long as you like, but still your physical life goes on—your heart beats, you breathe in and out, you are conscious of time going by. Afterlife time—call it A-time—need not be like this. We might have no sense of succession, of time hurrying by, unless we choose to.

So far so good. A pleasant prospect, you might think, being able to "reread" our good moments and "skim over" our bad ones. But we have not seen all the consequences yet of supposing that we might see these things in God, or as God sees them. For God, of course, would see them *as they are* without illusion or mistake. If our moment of triumph was flawed by pride or selfishness, we would see it so. If our "great love" was a romantic illusion, we would see it so. To see our life as God would see it might very well cause the bravest to quail, were it not that to see our lives as God would see them would be to see them in the light of perfect love and understanding. But we would see our sins too as they really are, in all their malice, in all their ingratitude, in all their ugliness. About this we might have no choice, and insofar as we can speak of one experience coming first in the afterlife, our first experience might be to see our sins in all their ugliness, just as God sees them. And since their full ugliness includes their effects on others, we might be granted knowledge of the lives of others to the extent our sins have damaged them. Even if Hitler had died repentant, his heavenly life might begin with a full realization of every evil he had done—the fears of every Jewish mother, the terror and bewilderment of every Jewish child in the gas chambers. If this speculation is correct, every time I hurt another person, his hurt lies inevitably in my future, to be experienced *by me* to the full.

What of those (and God forbid that there should be any such) who do *not* reject their sins? What if they see their sins as they are, know all the pain they have caused to others and still cling to them, because the sins are their own, their own creation, their own choice? This would be Hell indeed—to know sin as it is and yet to love it.

We have looked at the dark side; let us now look at the light. In looking through God's eyes at all of our sorrow and suffering, we would also see all the effects of that suffering on our own lives and the lives of others. Now religious believers have faith that no sorrow is useless, that no pain is unjustified. Then they might *see* in as much detail as they like how each sorrow that troubled them grew into joy for themselves or others. They would have all the answers to all the challenges of all the atheists who based their atheism on the sufferings of this world. And those atheists who also see that what they called Truth or Fairness was all the time a mask of the God who under other names they thought they hated.

But so far we have not yet explored all the consequences of seeing as God sees. To see as someone else sees is not only to see *what* he sees but also to know and share his attitude to what he sees. We would see with love even those who hurt us, because God saw them with love. We would see the fool and the bore in the full glory with which their Creator saw them. We would even see our foolish selves with that love and glory and begin to love ourselves as we should be loved. Each suffering, each frustration we would see as God sees it, as the only means to encourage a free choice for the good. Each animal, each bird, each stick or stone we would see as God sees it, in all the splendor His creative love gave it. Everything we had ever encountered, every person we had ever known we would see "by Godlight" and know them as we had never known them in life. It might well be as this process goes on that the whole of our past would begin to be continuously present to us, as the whole past of the world is to God.

When we had learned as much as we could learn from our own lives and all those lives which touched them, we would have the whole community of the Blessed to share experience with, all in the light of God. All art, all philosophy, all teaching and sharing would be just a pale shadow compared to that sharing, that communication. But all this would be just the beginning, just the prelude. "The enterprise is exploration into God." * When we had learned all we could from every created being, there would still be infinitely more to learn from the Uncreated Creator, from whom all these things came. When we had loved every created being as it deserves to be loved, we would have had a little practice for loving Love Himself as He deserves to be loved, a task which we would never complete.

Does this imply progress after death? Yes and no. Moral progress, no, for that implies a will genuinely free to choose evil, and if we reached heaven that choice would be behind us. But progress in knowledge and love, of course. How else could our finitude gain any measure of the height and depth and breadth of God's love without continually growing, limited at any given time yet never reaching an ultimate limit?

We will now try to answer certain questions which naturally arise if the eternal life view of time and immortality is adopted. But I want to make it clear that I am not claiming to answer these questions with any particular authority. My view of time and immortality is speculative; so is the answer to these questions. The best way to read these answers is as containing the rider: Granted the eternal life view of time and immortality, this to me seems a reasonable solution to that difficulty. Do you agree? Why or why not? How would *you* solve the difficulty?

The first difficulty is that this view may seem to be insufficiently

---

* "A Sleep of Prisoners" by Christopher Fry.

theocentric. After all, heaven is the state of being with God; Hell is separation from God. So why all the emphasis on our past lives and the events in them and our future relation to those events? The religious believer's answer to this difficulty is that our whole lives, past as well as present and future, have to be brought into relation to God and that a reasonable way for this to happen is some process of reseeing or reexperiencing our past in the light of God. The process of reading our past which we described was not intended as a substitute for being with God, but as a way in which our whole lives could be brought into relation to God.

A related difficulty is that if we in any sense see God or experience God after death, surely this tremendous experience would leave no room for interest in anything so relatively trivial as our past joys and sorrows. But it would be equally true (and equally false) to say that the love of God is so tremendous as to leave no room for love of our fellow man. As a pure mathematical proposition this is true: God is seen as infinitely lovable; the infinitely lovable outweighs all finitely lovable persons or things, so love of neighbor would be infinitely outweighed by love of God. But according to traditional Judeo-Christian belief, God *wants* us to love our neighbor; we *learn* to love God *by* loving our neighbor. So we would learn to experience God in Himself by experiencing Him in our lives and the lives of others, even in the afterlife. The relation of the sun to things visible in sunlight is a good analogy. We cannot look at the sun directly; we appreciate the beauty of sunlight by seeing *other* things by the light of the sun.

A question of a rather different sort is how much time this reading of our lives in the light of God would take, understanding that "time" here will mean something quite different from ordinary clock time. One plausible answer to this, in terms of a traditional Judeo-Christian belief in resurrection, would be all that period between our death and the General Resurrection, during which we would be disembodied persons; with the proviso that this period might seem no longer and no shorter to someone who died in the earliest stages of human history than to someone who died just before the General Resurrection. That is, the period of reading our lives in God would begin with our death and end with the General Resurrection, and though it might have some relation to the length of our lives, it would have no relation to the amount of clock time which elapsed between our death and the General Resurrection.

Before looking at other possible answers to this question, there is another related one: Why a General Resurrection at all? What need is there of bodies, even spiritual bodies, if the general picture of the afterlife we have given is true? A possible answer to this is that being the sort of creatures we are (men, not angels), a body of some kind and a common environment are necessary for us to communicate with other human beings. Thus the period of sharing lives and experiences might have as a necessary condition spiritual bodies and "a new heaven and a new earth." This period would have a natural end when all possible sharing had been done and would be followed by endless "exploration into God."

One note here: We are assuming that our A-time experiences could be ordered as being before and after certain events, but they would not necessarily be measurable by any kind of standard units between those events. Perhaps this would be more plausible for the period between death and resurrection when the soul is alone with God; it might be that if we then share a new heaven and new earth, we will also have to share some common measure of time.

We will next examine a group of less theoretical and more immediate questions, questions deeply felt by many ordinary people: Would we know our friends and loved ones? Would our relation to them be unchanged? What about children who die in infancy? Let us look at those questions in turn. As we have envisioned the series of stages, we would not be in active communication with our loved ones between death and resurrection, though we might be made aware of some of their pre-mortem experiences. But during the subsequent stages we would certainly be able to communicate with our loved ones, in a way which was never possible in this life.

Would our relationship to them be the same? That would depend on the relationship. If it was founded on genuine love and knowledge, it would remain and grow. If our relationship to a friend or relative was merely conventional, it might become real and loving, and if it was imperfect, it would be perfected. Indeed, our deepest relationships after death might be with those we had wronged or injured, when repentance and forgiveness would give rise to a special love. In that world, love of enemies would be the norm, not the exception.

There is a question of special importance to anyone who has lost a child in infancy: Will I know the baby again as a baby or will it be grown beyond recognition? If it is true that the experienced duration between death and the General Resurrection has no necessary relation to the clock time of this world, it would not be unreasonable to find such souls at the beginning of the sharing period still essentially child-like or even infant-like. By the process of sharing with this child-person, the parents might still in a way hope to bring up the child into an adult mentality.

The case of a beloved pet is a quite different one. We have no reason to suppose that in the case of an animal there is any self-awareness which could make survival after death meaningful or exploration or sharing possible. "The "immortality" that we could expect for beloved animals (or gardens, or houses) is the immortality of being present to us whenever we choose and known not only as we incompletely and inadequately know them now but, insofar as possible, with the complete love and knowledge of them which God now (and always) has.

Suppose that some souls survive, but are in some way damned or lost. (We may devoutly hope that there are no such and we are speaking merely of a possible but unactualized state.) Will they also have the power to read their past lives and enjoy past joys and triumphs? The answer might be yes, but there is a bitter paradox here. Insofar as the joys and triumphs of these lost souls were innocent and good, having as their bases love of God and of his creations, human and nonhuman, the lost souls would in the nature of their state now hate and turn away from those good things. Insofar as they would turn to the "triumphs" and "joys" tainted with evil, they would no longer be able to hide from themselves the essential emptiness and unsatisfactoriness of these joys and triumphs. Nor could they now believe that there are new triumphs ahead which will not be empty, the hope that often seems to sustain those who find that their earthly triumphs are empty once attained.

Another set of objections arises from the apparent unfairness in the distribution of benefits and sufferings in the world. The distribution of benefits does not seem to me to be a problem in the eternal life view, since by sharing, any of us would be able to experience whatever good any other person has experienced. But in the distribution of pains there seems to be a real inequity. Those who die painlessly in infancy would seem to be at an advantage compared to those who suffer pain for a longer or shorter time of life. Some of those who suffer seem to have offsetting advantages or enjoyments; some do not.

There is no avoiding the fact of unequal suffering. But does this inequality amount to an injustice? Granted, for the sake of argument, that all suffering benefits either the sufferer or someone else, it would follow that suffering is a *privilege* or opportunity for a person either to help himself or herself or to be a benefactor of others. Now the vital question is this: Would a just God be obliged to give each person *equal* opportunity to benefit self and others? Consider the possibility that God knows that some persons will make good use of opportunities granted, while others will not. Would it be unjust for God to give a privilege only to those who He knows will make good use of it? It would seem not.

Remember that we are not talking of what is necessary for salvation, but of opportunities for greater personal development or of opportunities to benefit others. It seems unreasonable to hold that such opportunities should in justice be given to those whom God knows will not make good use of them. It is often just for us to offer opportunities to all, since we do not know who will choose to take advantage of them. But God, in the traditional view, knows what will happen, even in cases of free individual choice.

We have put forward a view that life after death should not be envisioned as endless temporal succession but as an *eternal* life with three main phases: first, reading our lives in the light of God; second, sharing the lives of others; and finally, exploration of God. The first period might begin with death and end with the General Resurrection, the second might begin with the General Resurrection and continue until sharing is complete, and the third might begin then and never end. But none of these periods would consist of a given number of units of duration, and in particular there would be no necessary relation between the duration of the first period and the clock time elapsed between our death and the General Resurrection. Furthermore, in this view we would tend more and more to see our whole experience in one specious present, so that our whole existence, pre-mortem, and post-mortem, would be present to us at once. But this specious present would increase in a direction toward the future as we experienced more.

These ideas were put forward purely as speculations, but we will briefly examine possible philosophical and theological grounds for them, by trying to show that the eternal life view is a hypothesis which gives a satisfactory solution to a number of difficult problems in theology and philosophy of religion.

The first set of problems solved by the eternal life view is a cluster of problems associated with the traditional problem of evil, the objection to God's existence based on the apparently pointless suffering in the world. A real belief in a perfectly good and all-powerful God requires us to believe that there is no unjustified or useless suffering. Every bit of suffering we undergo must, if God is truly good, be of long-term benefit to ourselves or others. Yet it seems clear from experience that not all suffering is useful to ourselves or others in this life. Therefore, it must be useful to ourselves or others in the life to come. But in what *way* can present suffering be good for ourselves or others in the afterlife? Traditional views leave this dark, whereas the eternal life view gives an answer to it in terms of the reading of our lives.

Consider as an example a concentration camp guard in Nazi Germany who has terrorized and brutalized a number of Jewish women and children for his own pleasure and the sense of power it gave him. The guard is shot as the Allies liberate the camp, but as he dies he repents his deeds, and God in His mercy forgives him. However, can we really say that this man is ready for an eternity of happiness with God and with his fellow human beings, including those he has terrorized and brutalized? The traditional Roman Catholic view is that such a man is not prepared for heaven, that he must undergo the pains of purgatory before being admitted to heaven. This seems a rational solution to such a case; God, being pure Love, cannot give Himself to a man with unrealized and unrejected evil in his soul; the evil must be done away with before the man can be one with God. But how?

Here was the fatal weakness in at least some traditional conceptions of purgatory. It was conceived of merely as a sort of prison or torture chambers, and it is hard to see how suffering merely in and of itself can remove evil. But if a man who has made the basic decision to reject evil relived that evil, seeing it as his victims felt it, the man could then fully realize and fully reject the evil. The only adequate purgatory might be to suffer what you made others suffer—not just an equivalent pain, but *that* pain, seeing yourself as the tormenter you were to them. Only then could you adequately reject and repent the evil. This is an extension of the accepted Catholic doctrine, but in a direction foreshadowed by that doctrine.

Probably the strongest reason for the rejection of the idea of purgatory by the average Protestant is that perversion of the Catholic doctrine by which the rich man by paying for masses and prayers could be relieved of the pains of purgatory, while the poor man could not. But this *was* a perversion of the doctrine, and the essential idea that the love and prayers of our fellow humans (whether dead or living) could help us in our purgatorial ordeal seems reasonable. This is most obvious with the prayers and love of the victims themselves. But even the less personal prayers of those who love a particular sinner, or pray for all sinners, could be of help to them in purgatory, and in some way God might make the sinners aware of their love and support.

What about those sins of rage or hate or envy which harm no one? Our purgation for these might consist in seeing these as God sees them, in their full squalor and meanness and nastiness. Seeing them so, we could reject and repent. Many of our sins are such that it would horrify us if they were known to those we love and respect. But in the afterlife we would have to face up to the fact that God knew these sins in their full despicableness, and we too would see them so.

What about the victims, supposing them to be completely guiltless? They would rejoice in their sufferings then, because they would see the way in which those sufferings played a part in their own salvation and the salvation of others.

Of course, if the sinner did not "die in his sins" but repented and showed the fruit of repentance, he would himself have faced up to the horror of his sins, and felt an adequate sorrow for them and rejection of them. His total experience, then, in the afterlife, might be mainly of pardon and peace. He would have had his purgatory in this life not merely by suffering but by suffering for the right reasons and in the right spirit.

If a good God indeed exists, the logic of this argument seems inescapable; suffering is never useless but is always for our good or the good of others. If it does not do this good in this life, it must do it in the next. So far as we can see, suffering does not always achieve a good purpose here; therefore, at least sometimes the good must be done in the afterlife. The first good done would seem to be to make it possible for us fully to realize and therefore fully to reject our sins. God permits sin to result in suffering because only so can the sinner see the full horror of his sin. The second good done by suffering would be to make it possible for us fully to appreciate the love of others for us, and to love them in return. "Greater love has no man than this, that he lay down his life for his friend." But we do not always know or appreciate in this life the sacrifices of others for us. So we must know them hereafter in order to respond with adequate love and gratitude.

Some subsidiary mysteries would be solved by the eternal life view also. Why do some die young, some die in infancy, with no chance to appreciate the beauty of the world, the joys of love and friendship? In the eternal life view they are not deprived of a knowledge of these things but would receive this knowledge by sharing the experiences of others—first, perhaps by sharing with parents or others close to them in this life; later, perhaps by sharing with more and more of their fellow members of God's kingdom. Again, races or groups who have been deprived of good things of the body or mind or spirit would by sharing receive these, perhaps even from the hands of their former persecutors and exploiters.

A second cluster of problems possibly solved by the eternal life view has to do with the meaning or purpose of life before death. At the end of their lives people often feel a sense of frustration; so many good things have vanished into the past, apparently lost forever. So many mistakes have been made which seem now to be irreparable. If only they could live their lives over again, people sometimes feel, they could make a much better job of them. And to go on to a completely new and different life does not always seem to be an adequate solution to these problems.

Now in the eternal life view we would in a sense live our lives over—not that we relive them under the same conditions but make different choices—but that we would read them in the light of God and see the meaning of our lives. There might indeed be some things which we would regret, even reading our lives in God, but these would be things like injuries to others, and we would have all eternity to share love and forgiveness with these others. Even such regrets as not having traveled to a foreign country or pursued a certain career could be satisfied by sharing the experiences of those who have lived in or visited those countries or pursued those careers. And of course regrets about meeting or knowing others would be fully alleviated by the sharing process—we would have eternity to know more and love better our favorite saints or heroes, authors or artists.

Again, the reading analogy may be useful. On the first reading of some book we may appreciate only a little of its significance and richness, but subsequent rereading will enable us to appreciate the book more and more. And as we might write a commentary on a book that has meant much to us, so part of our afterlife could be an appreciation and correction of our present lives. Even if our present lives have been almost a failure—even if we are barely saved after a life of folly and waste—we could still make these wasted lives the foundation of something glorious—a "commentary" much better than the "book." There would be, of course, practical consequences of all this. We would not need to cling to our good moments nor regret wasted opportunities; nothing good for us would really be lost. And it would not just be something different, though better, which we would receive, but those very good things which we thought we had lost, seen in their real beauty and glory because they are seen in God.

As we conclude this book, we can ask ourselves what has been shown about the nature and justification of religious belief. We can see that religious belief has as its essential element a belief in some power which is superhuman, above and beyond human nature. The Eastern religions have tended to see this power as impersonal, while Western religion thinks of it as a Person, all-powerful and perfectly good; this view of ·God is common at least to Christianity, Judaism, and Islam.

Some belief about life after death seems to be present in most religions, but this is very closely tied in with the view of God held by that religion. The Eastern religions like Buddhism and Hinduism which tend to regard the highest reality as impersonal also tend to think of human personality as a limitation which must in the long run be done away with. The Western religions, again including Islam as well as Christianity and Judaism, hope for a personal immortality. Which view of immortality is taken will have profound effects on one's view of human life and human persons.

Eastern and Western religious beliefs are sufficiently different that arguments or evidence for one would not necessarily be arguments or evidence for the other, and indeed we have seen that Eastern religion tends not to be concerned with argument or evidence for religious belief. What have we seen about the evidence for religious belief in the Western sense—a personal God and personal immortality? Probably all particular arguments for religious belief come down to the claim that some set of religious beliefs is the only thing which can make sense of our total human experience. As G. K. Chesterton once said:

> It is very hard for a man to defend anything of which he is entirely convinced. It is comparatively easy when he is only partially convinced. He is partially convinced when he has found this or that proof of the thing and he can expound it. But a man is not really convinced of a philosophical theory when he finds that something proves it. He is only really convinced when he finds that everything proves it. And the more converging reasons he finds pointing to this conviction the more bewildered he is if asked suddenly to sum them up. . . . That very multiplicity of proof which ought to make reply overwhelming makes reply impossible. (*Orthodoxy*. New York: Doubleday and Company, 1959, reprint.)

Thus, all philosophical arguments about religion are to some extent partial and misleading, for we can deal only one at a time with what Chesterton called the "converging reasons" for religious belief. Perhaps the ultimate challenge of the religious believer to the unbeliever is the challenge to make sense of the universe without religious belief.

It is open to the unbeliever to answer that the universe does *not* make sense; that it is meaningless, absurd. But this answer cannot be lightly given. Whatever theoretical compromises may be arrived at by the philosopher who tries to show that the universe can make sense in the short run without making sense in the long run, most people will see the alternatives as exclusive. Either everything makes sense or nothing makes sense. And if nothing makes sense, then whatever practical arrangements we make to make ourselves comfortable or keep ourselves busy, our lives are ultimately meaningless too. Death will come to the human race as well as the individual, and all human hopes and aspirations will ultimately be as if they had never been; the story of the universe is "a tale told by an idiot . . . signifying nothing."

Sooner or later, in old age or sickness if not in youth and health, we must face these ultimate questions of the meaningfulness of our lives. Religion is the conviction that there are satisfying answers to these problems; philosophy of religion is based on the conviction that we should use our reason to examine the answers proposed by religion. If this book has started you on the long and difficult, but vital, task of rationally examining your religious convictions, or lack of them, it will have done its job.

DISCUSSION QUESTIONS

1. Do you think that there is a life after death? Why or why not?

2. What ideas do you have about life after death?

3. On what are your ideas about life after death based?

4. Would a view of life after death like that proposed in this chapter be satisfying to you? Why or why not?

5. What kind of proof or evidence could we expect for life after death?

6. Have your own religious ideas been affected by reading this book? How?

7. Can the universe make partial sense without making total sense? Discuss.

8. What criticisms of religious belief seem to you to be strongest? Why?

9. What arguments for religious belief seem to you to be strongest? Why?

10. How do your convictions about religion affect your own life?

SUGGESTED READINGS

BRODY, BARUCH A., ed., *Readings in the Philosophy of Religion.* Englewood Cliffs, N.J.: Prentice-Hall, Inc., 1974:

BRODY, BARUCH A., "Morality and Religion Reconsidered," pp. 592–604.

GEACH, PETER, "Immortality," pp. 655–63.

HICK, JOHN H., "Theology and Verification," pp. 315–30.

HICK, JOHN H., *Philosophy of Religion,* 2d ed. Englewood Cliffs, N.J.: Prentice-Hall, Inc., 1973.

Chapter 6, "The Idea of Eschatological Verification," pp. 90–92.

Chapter 7, "The Recreation of the Psychophysical Person," pp. 99–101.

YANDELL, KEITH, ed., *God, Man and Religion.* New York: McGraw-Hill Book Company, 1973.

HICK, JOHN H., "Faith as Total Interpretation," pp. 529–41.

Additional Suggested Readings

INTRODUCTIONS TO PHILOSOPHY OF RELIGION

FLEW, ANTHONY, *God and Philosophy*. New York: Harcourt Brace Jovanovich, 1966.

GEISLER, NORMAN L., *Philosophy of Religion*. Grand Rapids: Zondervan Publishing House, 1974.

MILLER, Ed. L., *God and Reason*. New York: Macmillan Company, 1972.

PURTILL, RICHARD L., *Reason to Believe*. Grand Rapids: William B. Eerdmans Publishing Company, 1974.

YANDELL, KEITH E., *Basic Issues in the Philosophy of Religion*. Boston: Allyn and Bacon, 1971.

MORE ADVANCED BOOKS ON PHILOSOPHY OF RELIGION

FERRE, FREDERICK, *Language, Logic and God*. New York: Harper & Row, 1963.

KING-FARLOW, JOHN, and WILLIAM CHRISTENSEN, *Faith and the Life of Reason*. Dordrecht, Holland: D. Reidel Publishing Company, 1972.

PENELHUM, TERENCE, *Religion and Rationality*. New York: Random House, 1971.

REICHENBACH, BRUCE R., *The Cosmological Argument*. Springfield, Ill.: Charles C. Thomas Publisher, 1972.

ROSS, JAMES F., *Philosophical Theology*. Indianapolis: Bobbs-Merrill Company, 1969.

ANTHOLOGIES

CAHN, STEVEN M., *Philosophy of Religion*. New York: Harper & Row, 1970.

DIAMOND, MALCOLM L., and THOMAS V. LITZENBURG, JR., *The Logic of God*. Indianapolis: Bobbs-Merrill Company, 1975.

DONNELLY, JOHN, *Logical Analysis and Contemporary Theism*. New York: Fordham University Press, 1972.

HICK, JOHN H., *Classical and Contemporary Readings in Philosophy of Religion*, 2d ed. Englewood Cliffs, N.J.: Prentice-Hall, Inc., 1972.

MITCHELL, BASIL, *The Philosophy of Religion*. Oxford: Oxford University Press, 1971.

Appendix:

A Capsule History
of the Philosophy of Religion

INTRODUCTION

While it would not be possible to give an adequate history of religion itself in the space we have available, it is possible to give a brief history of philosophical thinking about religion, especially if we confine ourselves to Western religion and philosophy. Understanding the history of philosophical thinking about religion enables us to put present problems into perspective, and see how present-day views have developed from earlier ones, but it can also remind us of problems and perspectives which are neglected today.

It is important to realize both the differences and the similarities in philosophy and religion at different periods of history. What is assumed or taken for granted changes from age to age, but once this is taken into account we can still regard the development of both philosophy and religion as a continuous change, not as a series of disconnected stages.

I. CLASSICAL ANTIQUITY

It must be remembered that in classical antiquity the question of God's existence was rarely raised in the modern way. The overwhelming majority of ordinary people believed more or less in a great variety of anthropomorphic gods and demigods. The few thinkers who rejected any religious belief were often reacting against the extravagances and absurdities of popular belief. Thus the philosophers who thought about religion had to think about the question of philosophy of religion in rather a different way than we are now used to. Instead of asking whether there is a God—an all-powerful, perfectly good Creator and Ruler of the universe—which is the natural question for moderns, they asked such questions as "Are there any gods?"; "If so, how many?"; "Are the popular stories about them true?"

The first philosophers to make major contributions to the philosophy of religion were the Greek philosophers Plato (427–347 B.C.) and Aristotle (384–322 B.C.). Plato wrote dialogues in which philosophical problems were explored and solutions to the problems were sometimes, though not always, offered. The principal character in most of Plato's dialogues was a fictionalized version of Plato's teacher, Socrates (470–399 B.C.), who had been condemned to death by the Athenians because his philosophical probings of their ethical and religious ideas disturbed their complacency. Plato used these historical facts as a framework for dialogues in which Socrates and his friends discuss such problems as life after death (in the dialogue *Phaedo*) and the relation of religion to morality (*Euthyphro*). In Plato's later dialogues, Socrates is no longer the principal spokesman, probably because Plato felt that he had moved too far away from the ideas of the historical Socrates. In one of these late dialogues, the *Laws*, some early versions of arguments for the existence of God in something like the modern sense of God are given, and the problem of evil is briefly explored.

God is spoken of by Plato as Spirit or Soul, and as originating change in the universe: an argument for Soul as the source of change in the universe is given in the *Phaedrus*. In another late dialogue, the *Timaeus*, something like a creation story is given, but since this is in the form of a myth or likely story, it is not clear how seriously Plato took this idea, and at any rate the demiurge, or workman, who is seen as forming the universe according to the ideal forms or patterns seems to be a subordinate being rather than a Supreme Being. In several dialogues Plato seems to teach a doctrine of reincarnation of the soul, but again in the form of myth rather than of argument.

Aristotle, in his work the *Metaphysics* also gives arguments for one nonmaterial being as the source of change and order in the universe, but Aristotle's "God" is not the creator of the universe; at least some sort of unformed matter is seen as having always existed. Also Aristotle's God seems (though the passages in question are rather obscure) to be unaware of the universe, since it would be beneath God's dignity to know a lesser thing such as the universe. In his work *On the Soul,* Aristotle argues that at least the thinking part of man (not the physical or even the emotional part) survives death and is indestructible. But where we have a feeling with Plato that his ideas about God and the soul had some religious or quasi-religious significance for him, in the case of Aristotle the arguments for God and the immortality of the soul seem to be merely scientific in the sense of providing theoretical answers to intellectual problems rather than having any significance for the living of life.

Of the classical schools of philosophy after Aristotle the most important for philosophy of religion are Epicureanism and Skepticism, which were critical of religious belief, and on the other hand, Stoicism and Neoplatonism, which both served some of the functions of a religion as well as being philosophical theories. Epicurus (342–270 B.C.) developed the atomic theories of Democritus (406–370 B.C.) into a full-fledged materialistic philosophy which left no room for God or the immortality of the soul: Indeed Epicurus claimed it as a major advantage of his theory that it released us from hopes or fears about the gods or about life after death. Democritus paid lip service to the common belief in gods, but argued that if there were any beings superior to humans, they must be material, and could have no interest in such inferior beings as ourselves. He also allowed the possibility of a soul in beings, but argued that it too must be material and able to survive separation from the body only briefly, if at all.

The Skeptics, who traced their origins to Pyhrro (360–270 B.C.), rejected religious belief not because they held doctrines inconsistent with it, but rather because they questioned the possibility of knowledge about anything. But since part of their skeptical method was to match opposing arguments on both sides of any question, the work of the skeptics has preserved some early arguments both for and against religious belief.

The attitude of the Stoics towards God and immortality was much more like that of the modern religious believer. We know the early Stoics only in fragments and quotations, but such later Stoics as Epictetus (A.D. 50–130) seem to have a trust in and even a love of God, something not found in earlier Greek philosophy. The famous Hymn to Zeus by Cleanthes (331–232 B.C.), another Stoic philosopher, might almost be a Jewish psalm or Christian hymn. The Stoics gave some arguments for the existence of one God and the survival of the soul after death, but these were basically versions of arguments given by Plato or Aristotle.

The Neoplatonists were a school of philosophers who developed some of Plato's ideas into a religious world-view. A major figure in Neoplatonism was Plotinus (205–270 B.C.). They held that a perfect spiritual being, "the One," generated a lesser being, "Soul" or "Mind," which in turn generated other beings until at length a being was generated which was far enough from spiritual perfection to be the source of matter which the Neoplatonists regarded as imperfect and even evil. In some versions of Neoplatonism there were as many as nine of these "Gods," each inferior to the one before. The Neoplatonists also taught the doctrine of reincarnation.

Neither Stoics nor Neoplatonists formed a religious sect or church in the modern sense: They were usually content to observe traditional and popular forms of worship of the gods, while giving their own interpretation of the real meaning of the stories about the gods. The Stoics especially were inclined to give allegorical explanations of the old myths about gods and demigods; for example, they saw the story of Demeter and Persephone as an allegory about the seasons. Something like this same attitude—observing forms of popular worship while giving the popular ideas a philosophical reinterpretation—is also found in Hinduism and in some nineteenth- and twentieth-century Christian theologians.

II. THE EARLY JUDEO-CHRISTIAN PERIOD

As long as the Jewish culture had comparatively few contacts with other cultures, philosophical thinking about religion did not develop within Judaism. But as the Jewish homeland was invaded first by Hellenic culture that was the aftermath of the conquests of Alexander the Great and later by the Roman Empire, the Jewish people were scattered over the Mediterranean world and subjected to close contact with Greek and Roman ideas even within their homeland. Thus in the several centuries before the birth of Christ we begin to find Jewish thinking about religion affected by such philosophical theories as Neoplatonism. Some Jewish thinkers—for example, the Alexandrian Jew Philo (20 B.C.–40 A.D.)—attempted to connect traditional Jewish monotheism with the ideas of Greek philosophy, and there was an attempt by some to explain away traditional Jewish beliefs by the same method of allegorical interpretation which had been used by Stoics and Neoplatonists for the Greek and Roman myths.

Christianity was in contact with Greek philosophical ideas from soon after its founding, and such early converts to Christianity as Justin Martyr (A.D. 100?–165?) began the process of applying the categories of Greek philosophy to the interpretation of Christian beliefs that reached its high point in the Middle Ages.

Within early Christianity there was considerable debate as to whether study of pagan philosophy and literature posed dangers to Christian beliefs, one party recommending the complete rejection of all pagan thought, the other hoping to "baptize" Greek and Roman philosophy and literature and use it in the service of Christianity. The first major figure to achieve a synthesis of Greek philosophy and Christianity was Boethius (c. 480–524), whose ideas remained influential throughout the medieval period, but an even more influential and long-lasting synthesis was achieved by St. Augustine (354–430), a powerful and original thinker, who passed through materialism to Neoplatonism and finally to Christianity. Augustine reinterpreted Platonic and Neoplatonic philosophy in terms of Christianity and was perhaps sometimes too much inclined to interpret Christianity in terms of Platonic and Neoplatonic ideas. In Augustine we find the first fully integrated synthesis of Christianity with philosophy; Boethius's philosophy seems not entirely Christian and his Christianity not adequately philosophical.

Augustine used Platonic arguments for the existence of God and the immortality of the soul; he also connected philosophical debates about fate and free will with religious ideas about human responsibility and divine grace and predestination. When the Protestant reformers rejected the medieval synthesis of philosophy and Christianity, they went back to Augustine as a source of Christian philosophy and theology, a move which had important repercussions on the development of Protestant theology.

At this period there was no corresponding synthesis of Jewish religious ideas and Greek philosophy—none, that is, which was acceptable to the majority of believers in Judaism. Attempted syntheses of Neoplatonism with Judaism tended to be more Neoplatonic than Judaic, and were rejected by most Jews.

III. THE MEDIEVAL PERIOD

In the Middle Ages a combination of factors laid the foundation for a period of remarkable development in philosophy of religion. Islam arose, flourished, and established itself politically, economically, and militarily. In many parts of the Moslem culture large Jewish colonies were almost always tolerated and sometimes respected. There were also Jewish communities in Christian Europe, usually tolerated but sometimes persecuted. Islam had overrun many parts of the old classical world and Moslem scholars rediscovered manuscripts of Plato and Aristotle which had been lost to Christian Europe in the Dark Ages after the fall of the Roman Empire. These conditions gave rise to a remarkable parallel development of religious philosophy in Islam, Judaism, and Christianity, which culminated in something like a philosophical synthesis agreed on by major representatives of the three faiths.

The major figures in Islamic philosophy of religion were Alfarabi

(A.D. 875–930), Avicenna (A.D. 980–1037), Algazali (A.D. 1058–1111), and Averroes (A.D. 126–1198). This brilliant succession of Islamic philosophers argued for the independence of philosophy from theology, gave arguments for the existence of God and the immortality of the soul, and tried to give philosophical answers to problems of free will, time, and the creation of the universe. All of them based their philosophical thinking to a large extent on Aristotle, but with a considerable contribution from Plato and the Neoplatonists. Some saw Plato and Aristotle as essentially in agreement; others criticized Plato in the name of Aristotle or Aristotle in the name of Plato. But although their philosophy often developed by commenting on classical texts, they had their own contributions to make. Alfarabi seems to have introduced the contrast between necessary and contingent existence, and Avicenna seems to have been the first to give an argument for the existence of God based on the idea that contingent being must be traced back to necessary being (see Chapter 4). Algazali was a critic of Moslem Aristotelianism, though very much influenced by it; he also gives an interesting discussion of mystical experience. Averroes, the last of the group, had few Moslem successors because of political and social changes in Islam, but he influenced Jewish and Christian philosophers, especially by his theory of knowledge.

The major figures in medieval Jewish philosophy were Saadia Gaon (A.D. 882–942), Solomon Ibn Gabirol (A.D. 1022–1051), and Moses Maimonides (A.D. 1135–1204). Gaon was influenced by early Moslem philosophy, Gabirol chiefly by Neoplatonism; Maimonides can be classed as an Aristotelian, though like his Christian peer Thomas Aquinas, he synthesized and systematized a great deal of previous philosophical thinking, classical Moslem and Jewish. Like the Moslem philosophers, the Jewish medieval philosophers gave philosophical arguments based on Plato and Aristotle for the existence of God and the immortality of the soul as well as discussing such topics as free will, Creation, and the nature and attributes of God. Saadia, for instance, in discussing the unity of God, criticized the Christian doctrine of the trinity as well as polytheistic or dualistic views. Gabirol's attempt to interpret Jewish belief in Neoplatonistic terms was not acceptable to most of the Jewish community, but Maimonides's great synthesis won wider acceptance and he came to be accepted as a major Jewish teacher, not only respected as a philosopher but quoted in the Talmud on a level with the great sages and interpreters of the Law in earlier times.

Medieval Christian philosophy began with the handicap of having less access to classical philosophy: At the beginning of the period only Aristotle's logical works and a few Platonic dialogues were known in Europe. However, medieval Christian philosophy was able to develop an ongoing philosophical synthesis which could absorb new ideas and new discoveries of classical ideas as they became available. It is this continuing community of Christian philosophy which we refer to as *scholasticism.* If we do not count Augustine or Boethius as the beginning of scholasticism, then St. Anselm (1033–1107), whose ontological argument we examined in Chapter 3, can probably be considered the first scholastic. While there were a number of important scholastics, probably the most important were Thomas Aquinas (1225–1274) and Duns Scotus (1265–1308), two men of wide ranging genius who, along with Maimonides, are the towering figures of medieval philosophy. Aquinas and Scotus attempted to build a philosophical system which took in Plato, Aristotle, the Moslem commentators on Aristotle, and the Jewish philosophers—especially Maimonides, whom they recognized as a major authority. Within scholasticism argument could go on within a framework of argument: Aristotle could be a starting point for argument with Islamic philosophers, and the Old Testament could be a point of agreement for theological discussions with Jewish philosophers, while Christian scholastics could agree on the authority of the New Testament and the early Christian commentators on it.

The characteristic medieval synthesis had a number of elements, some of the most important of which were 1) a distinction between philosophy seen as based purely on what unaided human reason could discover, and theology, seen as based on revelations from God, such as the Old and New Testaments; 2) a conviction that philosophy could go a considerable way to aiding religious belief, especially by proving the existence of God and showing us something about His nature; 3) the agreement that philosophical argument alone was not sufficient for religion, that revelation from God and a commitment to that revelation were also necessary.

It was this synthesis that was the background of much of the philosophical discussion in the Middle Ages; as we shall see, subsequent ages either rejected parts of the synthesis, or rejected it totally.

IV. SEVENTEENTH AND EIGHTEENTH CENTURIES

At the end of the medieval period scholastic philosophy continued to exist but, like many medieval institutions, seemed to lose its vigor during the period of discovery and turbulence which we call the Renaissance. This was not a period of great philosophical activity. As C. S. Lewis has noted, the criticisms made of scholastic philosophy by Renaissance thinkers were not philosophical criticisms, but rather criticisms which those with a basically literary orientation have always made of philosophy—hairsplitting, use of awkward technical language, etc. Around the beginning of the seventeenth century, however, two new and rigorous philosophical movements arose. In Britain *empiricism*—the insistence that knowledge is confined to what our senses can tell us—flourished, while on the continent of Europe *rationalism*—the view that reason is the source of knowledge—was dominant.

Two developments in British empiricism which were important for the philosophy of religion were due to David Hume (1711–1776) and to Bishop George Berkeley (1685–1753). Hume searchingly criticized traditional arguments for the existence of God and the immortality of the soul; his criticisms are still influential. Berkeley tried to draw new arguments for God's existence from a view which took empiricism to a logical extreme. If experience is to be our only source of knowledge, Berkeley argued that nothing can be known to exist but experience itself, and experience is a mental entity rather than a physical thing. In Berkeley's view, God had to be brought in to explain why we all have the same experiences of a world outside of ourselves: God is broadcasting the program of experiences we all receive.

In Europe the attempt to base knowledge on reason led to a revival of the ontological argument; Descartes (1596–1650) gave his version of it as we saw in Chapter 3, and Leibniz (1646–1716) gave new precision to Anselm's version of the argument. Spinoza (1632–1677) was a major Jewish philosopher, but his speculations and arguments led to a pantheistic view which caused his philosophy to be rejected by the Jewish religious community.

Toward the end of the eighteenth century Immanuel Kant (1724–1804) tried to unite empiricism and rationalism by giving a theory in which the substantial part of our knowledge came from experience but reason imposed certain necessary forms on experience. From the point of view of this theory, Kant criticized the traditional arguments for the existence of God; it is arguable to what extent his criticisms can really be defended apart from his general theory. As we saw in Chapter 3, Kant gave his own version of a moral argument for God's existence.

In general, the seventeenth and eighteenth centuries were a period in which philosophy of religion was on the defensive; even where new arguments were given for God or immortality they were thought to be necessary because the scholastic arguments seemed no longer effective. Yet at the end of the eighteenth century the majority of philosophers still retained the idea that argument and proof were possible in the area of religion. Indeed, there was some tendency to exaggerate the role of reason in religion: to restrict religious belief to what could be argued philosophically and to reject faith in the sense of reliance on revelation. This philosophical tendency, known as *Deism*, had considerable influence on the educated public in England and France, and also influenced several of the American founding fathers, especially Benjamin Franklin and

Alexander Hamilton. Some elements of Deism survive today in the quasi-religious aspects of Masonism.

V. THE NINETEENTH CENTURY

In the nineteenth century the empiricist tradition continued to some extent, especially in the American philosophical school known as pragmatism. But the major figure in nineteenth-century philosophy was G. W. F. Hegel (1770–1831), who was influential in a process of reinterpreting religion in philosophical terms, which continues today. This process was actually begun by J. G. Fichte (1762–1814), who rejected any attempt to prove God's existence from the universe and gave his own version of Kant's moral argument. But in doing so he *identifies* God with the moral order, and seems to identify that with something in human nature. Thus, God as separate from Creation disappears in Fichte's system; his view is at best pantheistic.

Hegel's key notions were the idea of development in general, and the idea of the development of the self in particular. The universe is seen as part of a process of development by which "Spirit," or "the Absolute," comes to a full realization of itself. At the end of this process the Absolute has many of the characteristics of the God of traditional Judeo-Christian belief, but the Absolute is at first completely without knowledge or choice, and develops through a process by which first animals, then human beings are the "organs" of its self-awareness. Hegel's ideas have much in common with earlier pantheistic views but added the idea of gradual development, which was extremely attractive to the nineteenth century, an era in which hopes for perfection by progress were strong.

The development of the individual Hegel saw as a struggle with, and an attempt to dominate, things and persons other than that individual. Both the Absolute and the individual person developed by a "dialectical" process in which a state (or "thesis") gave rise to an opposing state (or "antithesis"), and the two combined to make a new state (or "synthesis"), which was then the start of a new cycle. Karl Marx took over the idea of dialectical development as one of the key ideas of Communism, but left out Hegel's idea of the Spirit or Absolute, seeing the dialectic as a purely material process.

After Hegel, Ludwig Feuerbach (1804–1872) made explicit Fichte's identification of the moral order with human nature, and argued that religion is the relation of man to his own idealized nature, which is externalized as "God." Max Stirner (1806–1856) argued that if religion is reduced to this it loses all force and authority. This process by which the idea of God was reduced to the idea of something purely human has had very little subsequent influence on philosophy, but it has had a major influence on contemporary theology. The early demythologizers, discussed in Chapter 6, assumed a philosophical position of this kind; it was the philosophical motive for their demythologizing of Scripture. The recent "death of God" movement, discussed in Chapter 5, has also been heavily, though more indirectly, influenced by these Hegelian and post-Hegelian philosophies. The phrase "God is dead" was first used by Arthur Schopenhauer (1788–1860); he and Friedrich Nietzsche (1844–1900) developed their own views in opposition to those of Kant and Hegel: Both rejected religion and, in different ways, emphasized the human will as the basis of belief as well as action.

Some variety of Hegelian or neo-Hegelian philosophy was dominant in most universities at the end of the nineteenth century, but there were a few dissenting views of importance. In the United States, Charles Sanders Peirce (1839–1914) and William James (1842–1910) developed the pragmatic view, which connected truth with what works in practice; James's application of this to religion was an influential form of weak theism, which held that objective truth about religion was unobtainable but that it was justifiable to make a choice to live by a certain set of religious beliefs. In Scandinavia the Danish philosopher Søren Kierkegaard (1813–1855) reached similar conclusions on theological grounds: He rejected rational justification for religion and called for a "leap of faith." The general situation at the close of the nineteenth century, then, was that the dominant Hegelianism tended to explain religion in human terms, whereas the dissenting voices called for nonrational faith.

VI. THE TWENTIETH CENTURY

Already by the end of the nineteenth century some new movements were beginning in philosophy of religion. Roman Catholics began to revive scholastic philosophy, especially that of Thomas Aquinas. This movement was encouraged by the papal encyclical *Aeterni Patris* in 1879. In Protestant circles a reexamination of religious experience had begun; the ideas of Rudolf Otto (1869–1937) were especially influential. Otto argued that there was a basic human experience of awe and worshipfulness, what he called the *numinous* experience, which could provide a foundation for religion. Elsewhere in Europe and America new approaches to philosophy of religion were being explored. But the first important philosophical movements of the twentieth century seemed hostile to religion. In Vienna, after World War I a group of young philosophers who came to be called the Vienna Circle taught a philosophy based on the idea that the methods of science and mathematics were the final test of truth and meaning; on this basis they rejected even the meaningfulness of religious belief. Some members of the group had a decidedly anti-religious position, but it was the general position that science was the only arbiter of truth and meaning (discussed in Chapter 1) which had the greatest influence.

The ideas of the Vienna Circle were popularized in English-speaking countries by A. J. Ayer (1910–) and they found considerable agreement from Bertrand Russell (1872–1971) and others in England, as well as from the remaining American pragmatists. Thus a loosely organized movement called *logical positivism* or *logical empiricism* and based on the Vienna Circle position came to have considerable influence in English-speaking countries.

The Vienna Circle had been influenced (to what extent has been disputed) by the early ideas of Ludwig Wittgenstein (1889–1951), an Austrian who spent most of his later life in England. Wittgenstein came to reject his own early views and was influential in the development of *linguistic* or *Ordinary Language* philosophy in England: In the early stages this philosophical movement was characterized by the idea that many philosophical and religious theories arose from misuse or misunderstanding of language and that philosophical problems, including many about religion, could be "dissolved" rather than solved by showing the confusions about language which generated them.

This view was a two-edged sword: It could be used to attack religion by arguing that certain religious concepts involved concealed confusions about language, as in some of the arguments about disembodied survival discussed in Chapter 9. But the views of linguistic philosophy were also used to defend religion. Some followers of Wittgenstein argued that there are a number of different uses of language, each equally legitimate, and that religious language is one such legitimate use. But insofar as these claims could be made clear, they often seemed to amount to abandoning a claim of objective truth for religious teachings.

As linguistic philosophy developed, it abandoned some of its earlier claims about dissolving philosophical problems, but retained its insistence on clarity and its interest in the way language was used. The earlier linguistic philosophers had been uninterested in formal logic, perhaps as a reaction against exaggerated claims made for logical methods by the logical positivists. The next generation of philosophers, who now tended to call themselves "analytic" philosophers, felt they had learned from both the logical positivists and the Wittgensteinian and Ordinary Language schools of linguistic philosophy. Many of these analytic philosophers were defenders of religious belief and gave effective replies to old criticisms of religious belief as well as rehabilitating old arguments for religious belief.

It is characteristic of the delayed effect of philosophical thought on other disciplines that many scientists are currently influenced by the logical positivist view of the priority of science and that some "secular city" theologians have recently tried to rethink theology in light of early linguistic philosophy. Both schools of philosophy have been weighed and found wanting by contemporary philosophers, but it is not unusual for a philosophical view to have its greatest popular influence some time after it has been abandoned by philosophers.

Analytic philosophy is now the dominant philosophical view in the English-speaking countries and to some extent in Scandinavia, but the split between English and continental philosophy which began in the seventeenth century has perished, and the dominant philosophy in continental Europe for much of the middle twentieth century was some form of what can loosely be called *existentialism.* This term came into use after World War II in France, where novelist-philosophers Jean-Paul Sartre (1905–) and Albert Camus (1913–1960) taught a philosophy based on the ideas that the universe is absurd and meaningless, and that modern man is characterized by "existential anxiety" which is the result of this perception of the universe.

This form of existentialism was not only nonreligious but was even fundamentally based on a rejection of religious belief, as Sartre clearly saw. But Sartrian existentialism was linked to other views which resembled it. Gabriel Marcel (1889–), a contemporary of Sartre, was called an existentialist, though he rejected the label; Marcel, like Karl Jaspers (1883–1969)—a German philosopher who was also dubbed an existentialist—was a religious believer. Since Marcel and Jaspers emphasized the agony of personal decision and the feeling that human beings were alone and unsupported by God, they were called "religious existentialists" as opposed to "nonreligious existentialists" like Sartre and Camus. Existentialism was also linked to German *phenomenologists* like Martin Heidegger (1889–) and Edmund Husserl (1859–1938), who had emphasized the primacy of experience and questioned rational interpretations of experience, and to such nineteenth-century figures as Kierkegaard and the Russian novelists Dostoyevsky and Gogol. But by this time it was arguable that the term existentialism had been stretched so far as to be meaningless; it no longer stood for a philosophical view or method, but rather for a certain emotional reaction to the universe, a feeling of the absurdity of life and the agony of freedom. At any rate, contemporary German and French philosophy can no longer be described as existentialist: There have been some movements towards dialogue with analytic philosophy and a reappraisal of the nineteenth-century heritage. Sartre, for example, is much more Hegelian than was recognized when he was being linked to other existentialists.

I have not in this final section discussed the work of active philosophers. We are too close to the contemporary scene to evaluate it. In the Additional Suggested Readings which precede this section I have indicated what I think are some of the important books in philosophy of religion written by the present generation of philosophers. The present-day scene in philosophy of religion is lively and combative. Defenders of religious belief are no longer purely on the defensive; often the battle is carried into the nonbeliever's camp. But there are strong and well-entrenched criticisms of religious belief also, and the critics are far from discouraged. What does seem to be breaking up to some extent is a sort of "gentleman's agreement" to regard religious belief and non belief as equally rational and equally nonprovable. The next century of development in philosophy of religion may well be one of the most interesting in its long and varied history.

Index of Names

Index of Subjects